High Velocity ITSM

Agile IT Service Management For Rapid Change In A World Of DevOps, Lean IT and Cloud Computing

Randy A. Steinberg

www.trafford.com
North America & international
toll-free: 1 888 232 4444 (USA & Canada)
fax: 812 355 4082

Other books by Randy A. Steinberg:

Implementing ITSM
Adapting Your Organization to the Coming Revolution in IT Service Management
Trafford Press ISBN: 978-1-4907-1958-0

Measuring ITSM
Measuring, Reporting and Modeling the IT Service Management Metrics
That Matter Most To IT Senior Executives
Trafford Press ISBN: 978-1-4907-1945-0

Servicing ITSM
A Handbook of IT Services for Service Managers and IT Support Practitioners
Trafford Press ISBN: 978-1-4907-1956-6

Architecting ITSM
A Reference for Architecting and Building the Entire IT
Service Management Infrastructure End To End
Trafford Press ISBN: 978-1-4907-1957-3

Organizing ITSM
Transitioning the IT Organization from Silos to Services With
Practical Organizational Change
Trafford Press ISBN: 978-1-4907-6270-8

The average change request takes 9-22 business days to get an approval

35% of IT organizations report 1-3 major outages per week

70% of IT budgets are stuck in non-discretionary spend just to keep the wheels running

85% of IT organizations get blind-sided when new services go live

60% of IT organizations experience unplanned labor rates of 35% or higher

80% of IT organizations cannot clearly articulate their services to the business

6 out of 10 applications fail because they cannot be operated at acceptable cost and risk

Let's turn IT into a LEAN and EFFICIENT Service Organization!

- The Author

Dedication

This book is dedicated to those very hard working IT professionals, managers and executives who deserve to see their IT solutions deploy and operate day-to-day within acceptable levels of costs and risks to their company.

Table of Contents

Chapter 1

An ITSM High Velocity Overview

The Landscape Is Changing

IT is undergoing a fundamental change in how it manages and operates itself.

Without our realizing it, the primary role of IT as an engineering organization has been shifting from a primary focus on building solutions to one of integrating solutions from internal and external providers. From engineering to service integration. The practice of understanding business requirements, designing building and deploying IT solutions is giving way towards integrating pieces, parts and services together to meet those same business requirements. IT executives that don't understand this shift will face severe challenges in meeting business needs at cost and availability levels acceptable by the business.

The traditional IT operating model of delivering IT to the business in the form of bundled capabilities and assets is now wearing thin in an age of cloud computing, on-demand services, virtualization, outsourcing and rapidly changing business delivery strategies. The role of IT is rapidly changing from technology tinkerer to services thinker. Traditional alignment approaches are no longer enough. IT must blend with the business.

Many IT organizations have yet to recognize that the traditional IT operating model of delivering IT to the business in the form of bundled capabilities and assets is now wearing thin in an age of cloud computing, on-demand services, virtualization, outsourcing and rapidly changing business delivery strategies. The role of IT has now changed from engineer-to-order to service integrator. What IT traditionally engineered, built, owned and operated can now be bought from many sources more easily without inheriting the specific risks of ownership, support, building and managing an operating infrastructure.

The IT executive that cannot clearly articulate the services they deliver, the IT spend for those services, and how those services are consumed by the business is essentially running a commodity operation that is whip-sawed by business demand and will never been seen as nothing more than an overhead cost to the business.

At the time this book is being written, many IT organizations are still organized and operated as siloed engineering delivery and capability organizations. If the organization chart looks like the schema for a configuration database (e.g. application unit, network unit, server unit, etc. all reporting to an executive layer) then that organization may be in trouble. The forces of outside suppliers ready to provide hardware, applications, and network and support solutions quickly and at lower price points are growing at a rapid pace. IT will need to assemble services and solutions from many providers integrating these together in the optimum manner to meet business needs.

As many IT organizations are under great pressure to provide consistent levels of service with decreasing budgets, they often look towards rationalizing the technical and non-technical components that they control such as hardware, software, people and contracts. However, this approach can focus too heavily on the "parts" and forget that the business cares about the services made up by these parts. Many IT organizations are unable to accurately describe the business facing services they provide, the true costs of these services or how they are being consumed. Therefore, decisions on where to apply tight funds and how to take cost out are often made at the component level without a picture of the overall business impact.

To this end, IT is undergoing a fundamental change in terms of its expectations from the business and how it manages and operates itself. This change requires a transformation from a traditional focus on IT components and outputs (e.g. produce a report, install a server, implement an application) to a focus on business outcomes and value (e.g. reduce customer order wait times, quickly onboard a new employee, enable collaboration between internal employees and external partners, etc.).

There is a growing recognition that managing IT by technology fiefdoms no longer allows for the quality and agility expected by the business. IT must organize and operate by services being delivered, not the technologies being employed. A Services Thinking approach is critical towards helping IT transition to a service delivery organization focused on providing value to its customers at an acceptable cost and risk.

The transformation from engineering silos to services suddenly exposes a lot of waste. Much of this has been built up over many years. Services that are not cost effective, solutions that are over-architected beyond what the business needs. Slow delivery processes. Too many layers in the IT organization (when you operate by technology someone has to pull it all together so multiple layers historically have been created to "integrate" things).

A Services Thinking approach is needed and it must be a Lean one. Businesses are under greater pressure more than ever to move quickly or die. New technologies and business models can quickly put a large company out of business. For many years IT ran with the mantra "we are the business". Well guess what? A slow wasteful and costly IT delivery organization will no longer cut it in today's world. Solutions can't wait years and sometimes even months to deploy. IT must move fast. It must operate at high velocity. It must operate Lean.

New concepts and practices around Agile, DevOps, Lean IT and other approaches have been evolving in the industry to deal with this transformation. All of these offer great promise, but lack the Services Thinking approach that is so critical to success. It is painful to watch some of these evolve, dancing around the concept of services and service value in their own disparate ways without ever getting to the point. These practices hold great promise. The tenet of this book is that they are all tremendously useful, but they need to be integrated into an overall approach that delivers high quality reliable services when the business needs them. This book pulls all these disciplines together. They operate within the overall umbrella of ITSM. ITSM is the glue that holds them all together.

This book will directly address the activities, steps and approach for running IT through a program of IT Service Management operating at high velocity. Much attention is spent on where waste typically exists within an IT delivery organization. It then turns to what you can do about it. An overall ITSM High Velocity Operating Model is presented to provide a context for how IT operates in this new world. Critical practices such as Agile, lean IT, DevOps and other evolving operating strategies are presented in terms of their IT Service Management impact. Included are a set of tools that you can employ that can assist you in finding waste, operating lean and improving your own IT delivery execution.

Why This Book Was Written

If you read through this book and still don't believe there is a critical need for IT Service Management then good luck seeing if you can survive in IT for the next 5 years.

There is a lot of information out there in areas such Agile, DevOps, Lean IT and other disciplines. Much of it is presented disparately. Much of it is driven by IT development expertise which woefully leaves out a lot of operational needs and concerns. This book intends to overcome that gap. IT Service Management (ITSM) is used as the glue for pulling these disparate disciplines together. The all operate under an overall ITSM framework because it can't be said enough:

"There is NO value in IT to the business until the point that a service is actually delivered"

End of story. The business could care less about whether development is now moving to Agile, whether the latest technology has been implemented, or whether IT has hired the smartest people. If the service is down, IT hasn't done its job. If development delivers the code faster and on time, but it can't be operated day-to-day at acceptable cost and risk, then IT hasn't done its job.

Not to say that Agile, DevOps, Lean IT and other approaches are not useful – they are definitely important. But they need to be utilized and integrated into an overall approach that delivers high quality reliable services when the business needs them.

This book will pull all these disciplines together. They operate within the overall umbrella of ITSM. The ITSM High Velocity Operating Model describes how. Careful attention has paid to concepts like Agile and Lean IT and apply them to real world IT examples.

It is hoped that the content in this book can serve as a reference guide to IT workers, be they developers, IT support staff, executives, middle management or project leads who are working on IT initiatives to help make them successful.

The Business Case For High Velocity ITSM

At the executive level, focus should be placed on outcomes not the means to those outcomes. If executives agree to those outcomes, then ITIL™ (IT Infrastructure Library) and ITSM merely become the vehicles by which those outcomes will be achieved. The outcomes in most cases will center on cost initiatives and concerns, sometimes risk, very rarely quality by itself. Although people talk a good game about quality and certainly everyone nods their head about it, rarely are checks written for quality by itself unless it leads to lower operating costs or risks. Telling executives they need to implement ITSM or ITIL may get heads to nod, but rarely funds to be provided. Focus on business, cost and risk issues.

Another error IT frequently makes with executives is focusing on *IT total costs* versus *IT unit costs*. With this mistake, IT keeps focus on the total cost of computing (i.e. the IT expense last year was $400M) which management may view as too expensive totally missing the fact that the services and volumes that IT has to process may have grown because of business events. Worse yet, this focus keeps IT viewed as an overhead in the eyes of executives. It's quite possible (and highly likely) that ITSM can reduce unit costs, thereby allowing the business to do more at lower unit costs even though the total computing cost may be higher.

Selection of a return on investment strategy to take with executives will be critical. Below is a table that identifies several strategies that can be taken as you develop your business case:

ROI Strategy	Outcome	Examples
Cost Cutting	Eliminate and reduce IT costs for hard dollar savings	• Unplanned labor costs for time spent on incidents, fixing bad changes, dealing with bad releases, etc. • Unplanned expenses such as those incurred for capacity shortfalls, staffing shortages to meet demand • Services being provided whose costs exceed their value i.e. delivering email at $3,000 per employee per year • Assets that lie unused or underused such as unused storage, servers with low utilization, unused data center space or low virtualization of hardware • Bad outsourcing deals, wasteful licensing arrangements, inefficient sourcing decisions
Cost Avoidance	Implement improvements that will result in lower delivery costs in the future than those that would be incurred if not done	• IT unit costs to deliver service XYZ are $3,000 per employee for 1,000 employees at a total cost of $3M • Headcount will grow to 2,000 employees by next year increasing our total service cost to $6M • ITSM improvements will be used to lower our unit cost to $1,500 per employee – therefore the total service costs next year will be $3M for a savings of $3M
Cost Shifting	Shift costs from non-productive investments to productive ones	• 87% of IS budget is funded for maintenance and support activities – if we improve our process efficiencies, and eliminate low value services we can reduce that to 65% and shift those savings into new projects or offer better services

ROI Strategy	Outcome	Examples
Risk Mitigation	Mitigate operating risks that could lead to fines, penalties, bad publicity, loss of business, or customers choosing other providers	• Use ITSM as a means to implement a service "shield" or "buffer" between the complexities of IT service delivery and what the customers see and experience • Use ITSM to meet regulatory requirements such as COBIT, HIPPA or SOX or to avoid penalties • Use ITSM to reduce outages or improve the customer experience to avoid loss of those customers who may seek to get their services elsewhere • Use of high velocity ITSM practices to deal with suppliers and IT vendors that may already be delivering their products and services via the Cloud with continual release and deployment methods
Piggyback	Find a major project or business initiative that is already funded that could use ITSM to guarantee success	• Use ITSM to support a major business acquisition • Cloud computing initiatives cannot succeed without ITSM • Data Center move or consolidations • Large application development effort such as a new ERP system where there is a desire to build and operate with Lean, Agile and DevOps approaches
Market Capture	Implement operating improvements to compete in the market place	• Use ITSM to gain a competitive edge • Prove compliance to win a large contract or attract new customers – customers may specifically ask for ITSM on service bids and proposals • Use of high velocity ITSM methods to get products to marketplace much faster

Book Chapters in Brief

Brief descriptions of remaining book chapters are as follows:

Chapter 2 – The High Velocity ITSM Operating Model

This chapter presents an overview of High Velocity ITSM and its operating model. Provides a summary view of the model and introduces the core operating disciplines of Lean IT, DevOps, Agile, Integrated Application Lifecycle Management (ALM), Cloud Computing, Virtualization and Automation. It also covers some high velocity topics related to Service Transition such as Containerization and Declarative Configuration Management. It also stresses the importance of organizing as an IT service provider to truly gain high velocity ITSM objectives.

Chapter 3 – Lean IT Applied To ITSM

This chapter delves into using Lean concepts for finding ITSM waste. Presented here is use of the Eight Deadly Wastes framework cast into ITSM terms. Examples of waste typically found in ITSM systems is identified. Another example that highlights the concept of Cascading Waste is also discussed. An example of a software request fulfillment workflow is used to show how 4 key strategies for reducing waste can be applied to streamline that workflow.

Chapter 4 – Agile Principles Applied To ITSM

Use of agile practices pose interesting and effective changes in how solutions are built. This chapter covers agile concepts and strategies from the ITSM practitioner perspective. An agile operating model for ITSM is presented that illustrates how agile works for developing solutions. An example of how an infrastructure project can be done in agile as well as a maintenance and support effort is also discussed.

Chapter 5 – DevOps Applied To ITSM

This chapter covers DevOps practices from an ITSM perspective. Presented is an operational framework for working with development teams. This framework includes checklists for both development and operations staff for each ITSM lifecycle stage. It also presents a strategy for providing development staff with a catalog of operational services. Service offerings shown include some ideas for developer support as well as how operational services shown can integrate into the solutions developers are building.

Chapter 6 – Virtualization Applied To ITSM

This chapter provides an overview of virtualization technology. How it works, what it can be used for and what kinds of processing workloads work well or not so well with virtualized technologies. Included is a discussion on Change Management with virtualized devices and how this alters the risk profile when assessing change impact.

Chapter 7– Integrated ALM Applied To ITSM

This chapter briefly covers Integrated Application Lifecycle Management or ALM. Just as ITSM tooling suites synchronize and integrate many of the IT Service Management functions, ALM synchronizes and integrates many of the application development functions.

Chapter 8 – Cloud Computing Impact On ITSM

This chapter covers the basics of Cloud Computing. For ITSM, the Cloud represents a delivery channel for IT services. It is during Service Strategy that key decisions are made on whether to deliver services via the Cloud, which model of Cloud to use and who the Cloud providers will be. This chapter provides an overview of different types of Clouds and delivery models. It also addresses considerations for security and privacy.

Chapter 9 – Leaning Out Service Transition

This chapter directly hits where most of IT waste and inefficiency exist – the Service Transition processes. Here is where you will find ideas for how to deal with Service Transition in a world of rapid change. Covered are ways to handle Change Management in this world. Topics around Continuous Release, Testing and Deployment are included. Discussions of newer deployment mechanisms such as Declarative Configuration Management and Containerization are also presented.

Chapter 10 – Leaning Out Service Operation

This chapter runs through the ITSM processes of Incident, Request Fulfillment, Monitoring and Event Management to identify waste areas and solutions. Included is a program description for the 40-40-40 Problem Management Program to aggressively reduce incidents and unplanned labor costs.

Chapter 11 – Leaning Out Service Design

This chapter identifies cascading waste issues that are most prevalent with Service Design tasks. Presented are 6 strategies for helping IT identify their business services. Included are topics on where cascading waste is found, how Cloud site recovery is changing the IT Service Continuity landscape, considerations for high availability, supplier management and capacity sizing.

Chapter 12 – Leaning Out Service Strategy

This chapter presents topics on more effective management of the overall IT strategy. Presented here is a 5 step approach for developing an IT strategy aligned with the business. This approach has been used by a number of companies and is extremely effective in identifying service costs and seeing the impact of waste from a cost perspective.

Chapter 13 – Driving Out Waste With CSI

This chapter presents some strategies for operating as a Lean Service provider and establishing a Lean CSI Program. Describes are program approach, roles and responsibilities as well as governance. Included is a topic on how to break out of firefighting mode which is a common barrier to refocusing IT efforts towards operating Lean.

Chapter 14 – ITSM Lean Toolkit

This chapter provides a compendium of lean tools that can be used for analyzing, planning and identifying causes of waste. Each tool is described individually along with a step by step description of how it can be employed and what kind of situations the tool is best structure for.

ITSMLib Download Site

There are a number of tools that you may find helpful related to this book. These can be downloaded through a facility called ITSMLib™. This facility provides access to real world working documentation, templates, tools and examples for almost any ITSM project. The library is structured to easily find knowledge and can be easily searched with phrases and keywords to find relevant information. You may find this useful in jump starting your own solutions with ideas and content that has worked for others.

Here you can find many tools and aids that can help you jump start your ITSM efforts. Requests for access can be made to:

RandyASteinberg@gmail.com

When requesting access, please provide:
1) Your Name
2) An Email address
3) The company you work for
4) The country you reside in

This library is continually updated with content and we try to add things all the time as people see a need.

Chapter 2

The High Velocity ITSM Operating Model

High Velocity ITSM Overview

What is high velocity ITSM?

It is operating, governing and managing IT by service delivered with a keen focus on speed (velocity), efficiency, value, and cost. The focus on service glues together development and operations (utility and warranty) in a seamless solution. Continual Service Improvement is always in play, constantly looking for more efficient and effective ways of delivering defect-free services. Delivery is focused around service integration versus throwing technologies at the business.

With high velocity ITSM, IT is always on the lookout for waste. There is a constant look and re-look at how services are managed and delivered. How processes operate to manage and deliver those services. Are the most efficient means in place? Is waste eliminated? Can opportunities with virtualization, automation and self-service be exploited? Can delays and wait times be eliminated? Which activities provide value versus not? How to best handle activities that don't add value but still must be done? In short, how can we best make IT operate faster, leaner, and transparently at acceptable levels of cost and risk?

High Velocity ITSM Operating Model

Presented here is a model for operating IT Service Management activities with high velocity. The model uses the ITSM Service Lifecycle as a key foundation for how service solutions are strategized, designed, built, tested, deployed, operated and improved. With this model, the Service Lifecycle has been expanded to integrate modern core operating disciplines like DevOps, Lean IT and Agile. The lifecycle acts as the glue that holds those disciplines together.

11

The model is shown as follows:

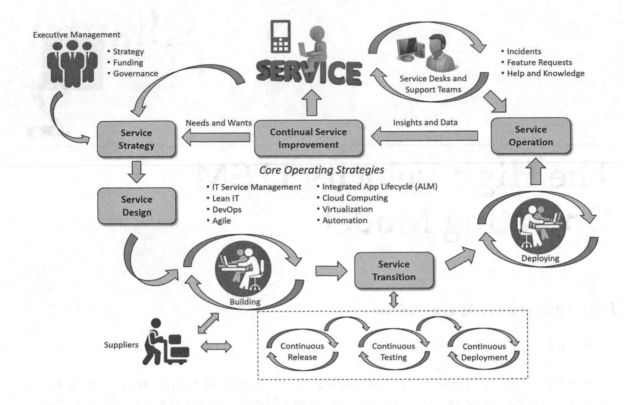

Core Operating Strategies

Let's start with the middle, the Core Operating Strategies. These represent key disciplines that will be utilized as part of the high velocity ITSM system. A brief description is presented below. More detail is provided in the next chapters of this book.

IT Service Management (ITSM)
It all comes down to the service. The business sees no value in IT until the point a service is actually delivered. The disciplines of IT Service Management (Service Strategy, Service Design, Service Transition, Service Operation and Continual Service Improvement) are more important than ever. ITSM is the glue that holds everything together. It runs from strategy to delivery and as can be seen above, forms the main flow of the entire lifecycle.

Lean IT
This is an extension of lean manufacturing and service principles to the development and management of IT products and services. The objective is to aggressively look at all the IT management processes and services and aggressively look for waste. There is a constant lookout for opportunities to become more efficient. This can include areas such as eliminating slow or inefficient process steps, automating common redundant tasks, increasing self-service, leveraging technologies such as virtualization that utilize physical resources more efficiently or Cloud Computing to eliminate the need to have to install and manage physical resources on business premises.

DevOps

A culture and practice that emphasizes the collaboration of software developers and IT Operations to allow for rapid and frequent build, test, and release of reliable software. Gone are the practices of throwing development solutions over the wall to IT operations. These forces now work in tandem at all stages of the development lifecycle to release solutions together. To deal with rapid change, continuous release, testing and deployment are in place. The objective is control changes and releases into the production environment, but do it much more efficiently such that the business does not get unnecessarily slowed down with long lead times to get new or changed solutions.

Agile

This is a solution development practice in which requirements and solutions evolve and continuously improve with rapid and flexible response to change. Agile practices focus on releasing fast with small increments of change versus large big-bang approaches. Rather than incur long wait times and asking the business to sign off on big-bang solutions, users get to see results much faster and provide continuous feedback that can be quickly incorporated into each agile release. Software itself is maintained in an agile manner, such that the latest release of software is always in production. This avoids lengthy projects and delays related to software upgrade efforts. Software defects are fixed much faster.

Integrated Application Lifecycle Management (ALM)

Taking a page from the ITSM community, the development community has recognized that you cannot continue to build solutions in engineering silos with myriads of disparate development and management tools that don't talk to each other. Activities such as version control, bug tracking, code management, project management, requirements tracking have historically been handled by individual toolsets. Tooling vendors have been aggressively looking at Agile and DevOps practices and are now coming out with integrated suites of development related tools that integrate development activities and information across the many development tasks.

Cloud Computing

This is about use of Internet-based hosting services to provide on-demand access to a shared pool of computing resources (e.g., networks, servers, storage, platforms, applications and services) which can be rapidly provisioned to achieve economies of scale. Efficiencies are created by having a 3rd party handle all the complex infrastructure management of physical resources, securing them and making sure they are available in the event of a disaster. Provisioning activities are done within minutes versus the typical 2-3 month timeframe to approve, fund, obtain, install and configure resources onsite.

Virtualization

Virtualization is about separating operating systems, data and platforms from the hardware they run on. Technologies have advanced quite a bit within the last several years to virtualize almost everything IT does that runs on physical resources. Servers, desktops, networks, storage and even data centers themselves can now be virtualized. While each choice taken here needs to be considered in terms of cost and risk, the advancements in this area should be continually examined. In today's world, it is not uncommon to see large amounts of servers, storage and desktops virtualized in many IT organizations.

Automation

IT automation is the handling of manual tasks through scripts and software in such a way that those tasks become self-acting. The benefits of automation are huge. It reduces or eliminates the need for labor, it responds much faster than people, it executes on tasks in a consistent and controlled manner and prevents errors and defects from occurring related to human mistakes. While ITSM may be the underlying foundation for high velocity delivery, it is automation that links everything together and makes it flow. Almost every task in IT can be looked at with an eye towards automation.

Included in the model is an expansion of the ITSM Service Transition stage. Concepts around Continuous Release, Testing and Deployment are used to vastly speed up the pace of change in IT services and solutions. More details can be found in the Leaning Out Service Transition chapter of this book. In addition, several key evolving industry practices are described that play a key role in speeding up Service Transition activities. These are:

Containerization

Initially used for effective and efficient application deployments, the High Velocity ITSM Model introduces the concept of deployment by "containers" for all infrastructure components that support services. Use of this executes deployments and request fulfillment activities faster, avoids human errors and simplifies Capacity Management activities.

Declarative Configuration Management

This involves taking advantage of new technologies emerging in the industry to auto-deploy Configuration Items. Rather than treat the practice of Configuration Management as a static provider of Configuration Information, this goes one step further and makes that information actionable. If all the attributes of a Configuration Item are already known, then why not pump those attributes into an automatic script that auto-deploys that Configuration Item?

The Model Lifecycle

Let's walk through the model at a high level. We will start at the upper left of the diagram and move counter-clockwise through each of the key elements.

Executive Management

It is here where key service decisions and strategies are made. What services should IT offer? How much do we invest and in which services? When should we invest? Are the services we offer in line with business goals and objectives? Are services delivering value? What kinds of projects need to be put into place to create, modify or remove the services being offered? Activities are strongly linked with Service Strategy. That strategy is represented and governed through an IT Service Portfolio.

Service Strategy

It is in this lifecycle step where the IT Service Portfolio is governed and managed. Executive decisions are made to determine where to invest, what projects to undertake or how IT will organize and operate to build and deliver services to the business. The outputs of this stage lead to projects that will build new services, modify or enhance existing services or remove services no longer needed.

Service Design

In this lifecycle step, activities take place to construct designs and specifications for building IT services. With a high velocity approach there is one key change here. Non-agile approaches might use this stage to build detailed designs that include every requirement needed by the business. With an agile approach, build activities proceed without knowing every requirement that may be ultimately needed. The business is not being asked to sign off on every requirement before build work can start. Therefore, this stage focuses at a higher level on things like Capabilities (What the service needs to provide), User Stories (discrete business needs/benefits) and service features that will be developed. These are then entered into ALM (Application Lifecycle Management) tools to kick off development team efforts. Larger efforts may include Release Trains which are combinations of multiple build teams that work together and release together.

Building

Solution building takes place here. DevOps practices are used to get development and operations to work together to develop comprehensive service solutions. Development teams focus on service utility – what features the service needs to have. Operations teams focus on service warranty – putting the infrastructure in place to make sure the service will be there when needed and will operate day-to-day at acceptable cost and risk. Suppliers are brought in to integrate their services with the solution being constructed. Build activities take place with agile disciplines. Solutions are released through sprints which produce production ready services in small increments of function on a frequent and regularly scheduled basis.

Service Transition

Here is where activities take place to handle testing, change, release and deployment tasks. While those activities are needed to manage and control what goes into the live production environment, there is one big change here. That is that those items now operate in continuous manner. Releases are always in play and managed through ALM tools that synchronize development code and branches. Testing operates continuously wherein new releases get thrown into the testing mix and thrown out if defects are found. Release to the live environment or staging area occurs at any time whenever testing activities have run a cycle without defects.

Deployment

Actions now take place to transfer solutions to user devices, workstations, system or other production environments. The mechanics of deployment leverage automation. Containerization and Declarative Configuration Management are used to automate and speed up deployment activities. Not all deployment will be immediate. There may be good business reasons to make sure that deployment does not occur during heavy business periods of activity (like a yearend closing) or that end users need to be trained. Sometimes logistics require that solution deployments be throttled back such as deployment of code to regions of the world that have network bandwidth issues.

Service Operation

In this lifecycle stage, solutions are operated day-to-day. Typical activities include handling incidents and problems, fulfilling requests, monitoring the operating state of solution components and performing administration and support tasks. Two elements make this one of the more important stages in the lifecycle. It is at this point that the business actually receives value from their IT investment. It also generates lots of insights and data around service quality, performance and business complaints.

Service Desks and Support Teams

These entities serve to provide contact points for the business to interact with IT to fix defects, fulfill requests and get help. Since the Service Desk is one of the first and main contacts between IT and the business, it provides a valuable resource for information around service defects, how services are being used and whether the business is truly finding value in the services they are receiving.

Continual Service Improvement

With this lifecycle stage, issues and defects are captured and analyzed for improvement opportunities. Insights are gained on how to execute services and manage supporting processes more effectively. Those opportunities are not just for application defects. A continual effort is made to reexamine how services are being delivered looking for opportunities to deliver faster and at lower cost. A Continual Improvement Register is kept to list these opportunities. This is shared across IT and with executives who may use that information to tweak and tune their strategies.

Organizing As An IT Service Provider

You can't solve the issues of higher operating velocity purely through newer technologies and processes. IT also needs to organize as a service provider.

IT cannot manage itself as it has in the past primarily by technology silos in a world where services depend on a well-coordinated chain of delivery technologies individually managed by those silos. The service is the sum of what is delivered from all the technology silos that support it. If one silo fails, the service fails. Therefore, accountability needs to be built into the organization for the overall service.

Without this, it is IT executive leadership that is stuck providing the coordination and integration points to get services to work. This is a situation that IT leaders constantly complain about. Why can't IT get its act together? Why do they have to be on the phone over and over to many IT support teams just to get things done?

Even worse, what happens if IT leadership itself abandons the role of service integration? The result is not pretty. At that point, the business ends up performing coordination and integration activities just to make sure their services will deliver. Their view of IT will be very low ("they can never get anything done" they will say) and satisfaction with IT services will be at a horrible level.

Therefore, the need for service integration is always there whether IT wants it or not. If IT operates in a way that is inconsistent with service management, then those activities will drift upward towards the business. If the business feels they need to take over those activities, they will go out and buy their own tools and services outside of the IT organization.

Operation of services delivered at high velocity must include the structure of an IT organization that is focused and accountable for services. Organizing around technologies and capabilities is not enough. Imagine running an Agile Scrum session and there is no Product Owner? Imagine operating in the role of CIO and there is no one to turn to when a key service goes down?

Accountability for each service needs to be in place. IT career paths need to diverge allowing for technology specialists who understand how things work on an equal footing with those who understand how to bundle and integrate disparate technologies and service offerings from others into a seamless service that customers can understand and consume.

The role of Service Owner is the most important organizational change needed to be successful. With this role, a Service Owner is accountable end-to-end for delivery of the service. If the service experiences an incident, it doesn't matter where the root cause lies or which team needs to be called in. The service is still out and it is a Service Owner responsibility to get the service back up, even if that includes coordinating with many teams to make that happen. No more pushing tickets back to the Service Desk!

The Service Owner role should be established at an organization level that allows them to interoperate across existing support teams and technology silos. It is suggested that this role be placed within a new organization silo that reports directly to IT executive leadership. As an alternative, this role could exist within a logical organization structure drawn from the existing silos. In this case, the logical organization has a direct line to the IT executive leadership.

The Service Owner role not only provides a single point of contact function for a service, but also works to improve service delivery performance. Broad-based measures that cut across technology silos are used to gauge service performance. The failing of one or more technology silos no matter where they exist will be reflected in the incident counts, problem counts, service breaches and delivery measures for the service as a whole.

The Service Owner should be accountable for how well the service performs. Include in their job description the responsibility accountability for taking action when service performance is out of spec or trending out of spec. Give them organizational power. For example, they should have access to senior leaders, involvement in all major and monthly review meetings, budget control, a title, and a say in rewards and incentives for line managers.

Secondary to the Service Owner role is the role of Business Relationship Manager (BRM). This role provides the voice of the customer view on service delivery activities, customer requirements, needs and wants. It is critical to communicating with the business. BRMs can be either in IT or in the business units. They are accountable for IT meeting business unit needs.

Organizing as an IT service provider is discussed at length in the Organizing ITSM book. In that book you will find recommended roles and responsibilities and examples of organization structures for different delivery models.

The key takeaway from this book should be the concept that organizing as a service provider is key and ensure that an acceptable organizational solution is considered to be truly high velocity. This cannot be covered over with different processes, tools or use of leading agile practices.

Chapter
3

Lean IT Applied To ITSM

Lean IT Overview

Applying Lean concepts to ITSM is about eliminating waste throughout the IT organization. Waste results in higher operating costs due to unplanned labor activities, rework, and delays. It takes IT labor focus away from projects that will move the business forward and ties it down to reactive fix and repair activities. Lean concepts have been around for years, primarily in the manufacturing industry. The objective of this chapter is to take those same concepts and apply them to IT. By doing this, IT resources and labor can focus on activities that truly help end users, impact the business, and grow the bottom line.

Lean IT promises to identify and eradicate waste that otherwise contributes to poor customer service, lost business, higher than necessary business costs, and lost employee productivity. To these ends, it targets eight elements within the IT enterprise that add no value to the finished product or service or to the parent organization.

To accomplish Lean IT objectives, the Eight Deadly Wastes tool (See Lean Toolkit chapter for more detail) will be used to provide a general framework for looking at waste within a Service Management system. The framework will be used to identify where IT waste is typically found and what opportunities might exist to remove that waste.

This means applying each of the waste categories from the Eight Deadly Wastes tool to the services, the IT organization is delivering. Each service, service lifecycle process, application, request and operational workflow, infrastructure area and development component is assessed against each of the eight waste categories.

For each category, this chapter provides a small list of typical IT ways of operating that might be starting points for finding waste. A list is presented for each waste category. While nowhere complete, it is hoped that the items listed provide enough hints to help you find waste within your own IT organization.

A Framework For Finding Waste

The framework is shown below:

	Type Of Waste	Description
	Inventory	Excess products and materials that are not being used
	Talent	Improper or inefficient use of people skills and knowledge
	Waiting	Wasted time waiting for the next step in a process
	Motion	Unnecessary movement of people
	Defects	Efforts to fix data errors, program bugs or other types of failures
	Transportation	Unnecessary movement of data or outputs
	Overprocessing	Producing at levels of quality more than required by the customer
	Overproduction	Creating more output than what is needed or before it is needed

The types of waste listed in the table above are pretty typical of most Lean programs found in manufacturing and other industries. They also easily apply to IT. Let's look at each one individually and see how these kinds of wastes are typically found throughout almost any IT organization.

Waste Category #1 - Inventory

This refers to excess product and materials for which labor or other resources is being expended yet those items are not being used. ITSM related examples of this kind of waste can include:

- Production of system documentation that is never used by IT support staff
- System resources that are running at low utilizations (e.g. storage pools where only 5% of that resource is actually used, servers and network lines that are running at utilization rates below 15%)
- Software license agreements where large numbers of licenses have been purchased but only a small number are being used
- Application software that is being built or purchased, yet not really used

- Data Center facilities where less than half the floor space is used
- Development teams that are sitting idle
- Services being provided and managed that no one really cares about
- Poor scheduling and leveling of IT resources to meet service demand volumes
- Staff work areas that are half-empty and under-utilized.

Keep an eye out for anything tangible that appears to not be in use or for items being produced that no one uses. Focus on sizeable opportunities. Inventory waste is one of the easiest things to fix and can provide significant early wins in your efforts. Some challenges might exist with individuals who may want to hold onto their pet projects and resources. Making the cost savings public is a good way to overcome those challenges.

Waste Category #2 - Talent

This refers to a misuse of people and skills. ITSM related examples of this kind of waste can include:

- Spending a majority of staff labor on reactive and unplanned non-value tasks (e.g. fixing incidents, bad changes, rework) versus proactive improvement projects or building new services
- Spending large amounts of time researching issues and obtaining information because knowledge wasn't readily available
- Staff resources assigned to projects that no one cares about
- Use of expensive resources doing common IT tasks that lower cost labor resources could handle (e.g. too many requests or incidents are being escalated to Level 2 staff when Level 1 staff could easily handle given proper training or knowledge)
- Not taking advantage of the full set of skills and experience of existing support or development staff (e.g. may have an individual with 2 Masters degrees working as a Service Desk analyst)
- Utilizing development and support resources that are under skilled for the tasks they need to undertake
- Poor retention of skilled resources
- Staff resources spend inordinate amounts of time on mundane or repetitive tasks that could be better automated
- Failing to capture good ideas and innovation from support and development staff
- Major incident process that requires all support resources to be on a bridge call when in reality only 2 people are doing most of the talking
- Meetings that take place week after week that provide little value yet consume lots of resource time
- Use of less skilled resources on tasks that require highly skilled resources that could result in those tasks being done much more slowly or with errors

- Failing to obtain support staff points of view on how issues and problems might be best addressed or where they may see efficiencies that could be implemented.

With this category, examine how staffing resources are being used. Do they have additional talents and skills that could be employed on other initiatives that could provide value? Are they being challenged to provide ideas and solutions that would allow IT to operate more efficiently and at lower costs and risks? Are expensive resources being used where lower cost resources may be able to provide similar outcomes? Is too much time being diverted to unplanned work away from projects and initiatives that could provide more value?

Waste Category #3 - Waiting

This category refers to lead time where a process is simply wasting time waiting to get to the next step in the process. ITSM related examples of this kind of waste can include:

- Change management process where 80%+ of the time is spent waiting for approvals to happen
- Software provisioning process where days or weeks are spent waiting for approvals to get the software
- Scheduling constraints that push back target dates and deadlines because reviews, implementation and fulfillment tasks couldn't be scheduled in line with target outcome timeframes
- Server provisioning times that take weeks or even months waiting for a technical support resource to get assigned
- Large scale deployments where sites may have to wait months or even years to get a new or upgraded solution
- Waiting to reach a Service Desk representative to handle a situation which could easily be done via a self-service facility
- Holding back on development progress until every possible business requirement is identified and waiting until the business signs off on all the requirements
- Finger pointing across the IT organization as to who is responsible for support, provisioning or request fulfillment activities
- Holding off on release of a new application or service until every possible feature is put into the release
- Holding off on a release of a new application or service until it passes a lengthy battery of test runs and quality assurance reviews
- Fulfilling requests in serial fashion versus batching up requests to possibly handle them all simultaneously
- Long queue times that are the result of not enough resources to handle the workload demand placed on them
- Delays caused by escalation of support tickets (incidents and problems) to other support staff

- Delays caused by waiting for too many decisions to be made (e.g. staff not empowered to make decisions, therefore management becomes a bottleneck to get timely decisions made).

With this category, hone in on places where unnecessary delay time occurs waiting for something. Examine each place where a queue, signoff, approval, or decision is required. Are these really necessary? Can work be batched to handle multiple things at the same time or must each task wait until the next one finishes? If wait times need to occur, can they be minimized? If large scale deployments are taking place, can these be done more simultaneously versus one site after the other?

Waste Category #4 - Motion

This category refers to unnecessary movement of people. ITSM related examples of this kind of waste can include:

- Dispatching support services out to local sites when the work could be done remotely
- Utilizing support staff to handle tasks that could be automated
- Flying staff or managers out to locations to attend meetings when those meetings could be held virtually without the need for travel
- Locating IT staff resources physically far from their management or others they need to frequently communicate with such that staff need to travel from one end of the campus to another to hold frequent meetings
- Excessive efforts spent to search for information such as configuration settings, knowledge, hardware and software inventories
- Chasing down approvals where multiple parties need to be involved in the final decision
- Re-solving incidents over and over because diagnostic and work-around solutions have not been published or communicated
- Chasing down approvals that are not really necessary
- Locating staff resources in facilities are locations that are far from basic resources such as food, parking or bathrooms that consume large amounts of time to get to
- Not providing enough meeting space or conference rooms such that meetings and activities get delayed until those facilities become available (e.g. "we can't meet at 9am as no rooms are available until after 2pm...").

With this category, look at people in the IT organization and how they physically move around. Are large chunks of time spent going out to lunch because there is no cafeteria nearby? Are people constantly traveling from one end of the building or campus to the other because they are in disparate locations? Is work being done onsite that could be done remotely? Unnecessary motion can really chew up time. Be on the watch not only for those situations that require long travel, but also for small amounts of time that are wasted in this category that occur frequently. It may take only 5 minutes to walk down to the manager's office, but if this happens ten times a day that adds up to almost an hour a day, 5 hours a week, 20 hours a month or 240 hours a year. That's almost 6 weeks out a year wasted!

Waste Category #5 - Defects

Perhaps no other category wastes more time and resources in IT than this one. Defects result in unplanned labor to address. They impact not only the flow of work in the IT organization, but also flows of work within the business itself. If serious enough, they erode business confidence in IT capabilities and can even impact business customers and the reputation of the business itself. ITSM related examples of this kind of waste can include:

- Incidents and problems that disrupt applications, infrastructure and services
- Failed changes that disrupt production
- Releases that contain program errors and application bugs
- Solutions that may work, but still fail to meet customer requirements
- Unfilled service expectations caused by lack of awareness of what those expectations should be
- Slow application response times that frustrate business users
- Inaccurate data that is being produced
- Defects caused by unauthorized system and application changes
- Defects caused by poor project execution
- Defects caused by poor product designs
- Development of applications and services that are not fit for use by the business
- Defects caused by services that cannot be operated day-to-day at acceptable cost and risk
- Failed deployments
- Services and applications put into production that introduce security risks
- Delivering solutions that are not meeting business needs
- Improperly deploying services into production that are not operationally ready
- Defects that are discovered late in the solution development or transition cycle such that they are much more expensive to fix than if they had been found earlier.

With this category, look around IT for where defects occur. Incident tickets make a great start. Categorize these (if not properly categorized already) to hone in on areas that might be addressed. Unplanned labor is also another good metric to look at. Another is what happens when a new release goes live. If introduction of new applications and services causes higher rates of incidents and support confusion, then opportunities may exist to remove this waste through a better release or operational readiness process.

What percent of the time do people spend fixing and repairing incidents and issues versus working on projects and improvements? If that time is significant, eliminating defects may carry a lot of value.

Waste Category #6 - Transportation

This category covers waste found in unnecessary movement of data or outputs from a process. Many times in IT, data is needlessly moved around from one system to another. Forms that are filled out manually might be rekeyed into an IT system. ITSM related examples of this kind of waste can include:

- IT systems where data is created in one system and then moved to another system in order to support a service or business function
- Asking users to manually fill out a form and then manually rekeying the filled out form into an IT system
- Deploying desktop images from a central source to a large number of desktops located at remote sites versus deploying to a much smaller number of image servers located at sites where those desktops exist and then letting desktops pull from their local server
- Deploying entire images versus just the applications and components that have actually changed
- Having to physically observe, count and audit hardware and software for compliance with asset and security policies
- Having end users ship their desktops into a central depot facility in order to get them repaired and then having to wait until the repaired desktop is shipped back to them (why not just ship a spare desktop as soon the user reports an issue?)
- Allowing users to store data on personal hard drives which then takes hours, days or even weeks to recover when they get a new or repaired desktop
- Systems that produce CSV (Comma, Separated Value) files or other output formats unnecessarily in order to feed that output into another system
- Managing pools of physical servers which have to be manually commissioned and decommissioned versus leveraging use of virtual servers
- Applications that create temporary work files on inefficient media such as tape, disk, or CD versus using memory or electronic storage
- Managing, configuring and deploying physical desktops versus leveraging virtualized desktop technologies
- Running sub-optimized network configurations that make movement of data occur over too many hops and routes
- Needlessly batching outputs when these could be input directly to the next system in the workflow
- Mailing or even emailing reports to end users when these might be better viewed in a shared portal or dashboard.

Similar to the Motion Category, examine each place where data is being moved from one system to the next. Is this really necessary? Are forms and data being reformatted or rekeyed in order to move from one system to the next? Could the production of data from one system directly flow into another system?

Waste Category #7 - Overprocessing

This category addresses processes and tasks that spend resources, time and effort delivering far above what is needed. ITSM related examples of this kind of waste can include:

- Applications that are constructed to deliver many more features than what the business has asked for
- Excessive documentation and review procedures
- Using forms and screens that slow down users because they force formats that are unnecessary or could be determined in the background (e.g. forms where the user has to enter their phone number one number at a time into a series of formatted boxes – why not just give them a blank box to enter their number?)
- Buying and using software that is overkill for the functions that were originally required (e.g. purchased an expensive configuration management database system just to keep inventories of hardware and software)
- Operating with multiple tools that all do similar functions
- Forms and screens that ask for much more information than what is needed to accomplish their mission (e.g. does a password reset request really need 3 pages of detail filled out?)
- Using multiple tools to provide the best of breed across every function needed versus a single tool that provides the basic needs across all those functions (e.g. use of multiple monitoring tools because different products are best of breed on different operating systems and networks)
- Tracking assets and configurations down the minutest detail when no one cares or it is not cost effective to do so (e.g. tracking PC cords, cables and mice into an asset tracking system which adds considerable administrative overhead when in reality, these items can be cheaply replaced)
- Delivering IT services that are seldom used or no one really cares about
- Solutions that are crafted to include and handle every possible exception that might occur
- Implementing custom solutions when off-the-shelf solutions already deliver most of what is needed
- Implementing a stringent change management process and set of controls to handle low risk/low impact or standard changes
- Running a long set of comprehensive and stringent applications test cycles on an application that has low risk/low impact to the business organization
- Delivering IT services that cost much more to operate and deliver than the value that they actually provide.

IT historically goes for perfection. Many times there is the thinking that unless every business requirement, function or feature is implemented the solution will not be acceptable. It is easy to over-architect solutions and build much more than what the business would be happy with. Constructing more than what is really needed is a form of waste. It is not unusual to find millions of dollars in IT solutions that are over-architected, expensive to operate, and cost much more than the value they provide to the business. Examine each solution delivered by your IT organization to look for potential opportunities in this category.

Waste Category #8 - Overproduction

While the Overprocessing Category focuses on systems and services that have been implemented with more functions and features than necessary, this category focuses on whether the outputs from applications and services produce more than necessary. ITSM related examples of this kind of waste can include:

- Operating with more network, storage, memory or processing capacity than what is really needed or actually used

- Overproduction of outputs related to poor customer communications or definition of requirements

- Production of reports and dashboards that no one uses or looks at

- Screens and forms that are seldom used

- Delivery of low value applications and services

- Reports and dashboards that include many more metrics and information than what people need or see value in using

- Reports, dashboards, service catalogs and portals that provide much more detail and information than what is really needed

- Implementing software patches and updates that may not be needed

- Producing system documentation, user guides or other form of documentation that provide much more than the recipients of those items needs to know

- Providing too many emails and communications about the status of user requests

- Producing monitoring and event data with details far beyond what most support staff need or look at

- Services that being delivered at higher service targets than what was originally agreed to through SLAs or other agreements

- Level 2 support staff that responds directly to end user calls to resolve issues or fulfill requests that never go through the Service Desk

- Collecting and recording log data at intervals that are much more discrete than what is needed (e.g. logging server activity every second versus once every 2 minutes)

- Providing state-of-the-art customer care at the Service Desk when only basic call handling and support functions are needed.

Similar to the Overprocessing Category, examine each service, system, application or infrastructure that is in place to see if it is delivering at levels needed by the business. Delivering more than what is needed is not necessarily a good thing. Those extra items can cost more in resource and labor, set the wrong expectations with users and take resources away from more valuable projects and improvements.

Cascading Waste

Don't just look at waste categories previously described by themselves. Sometimes combinations of those categories can create even more significant amounts of waste. A domino effect can occur where the occurrence of one form of waste in one category can cause another form of waste in another category. This is known as cascading waste. Consider the following example:

- Defective server hardware (Defects) may cause a major incident service outage that in turn causes a lengthy wait for users of that service (Waiting)
- This results in excessive demand on the Service Desk (Motion)
- The excessive demand elongates the call and dispatch queues (Waiting)
- More Service Desk agents are brought in to deal with the demand (Inventory)
- The impact is such that senior management needs to get involved (Motion)
- Skilled resources need to drop projects they are working on to address the incidents (Talent)
- The business now uses manual work arounds to deal with their customers (Motion)
- IT Business Relationship Managers are dispatched to business locations to quell concerns about service availability (Transportation)
- Server architectures are updated with duplicate servers and failover capabilities to avoid the incident in the future (Overprocessing and Inventory)

Perhaps upgrading server hardware in the first place might not be quite so expensive when you consider the impact of cascading waste!

Leaning Out Processes

Much has been said in this book about how to identify waste in an ITSM system. This chapter now addresses some strategies for dealing with it.

- **Focus On Each Process** – what steps provide value? What steps introduce delays? (e.g. 90% of change management time is spent waiting for an approval, users wanting software wait days or weeks to get approvals – why not give it to them right away and the revoke later if not authorized?

- **Automate Common Tasks** – institute an aggressive automation program to automate common fulfillment tasks and/or reduce human engagement

- **Increase Self-Service** – extend portals and the IT Service Catalog to allow users to engage more and more with IT self-service

- **Leverage Virtualization** – virtualize servers and PCs to speed up provisioning activities and provide more efficient management and support

When looking at a process to make it more efficient, here are some key strategies you might employ:

Strategy #1 – Eliminate Unneeded Process Steps

With this approach, lay out each process in terms of its steps, identify which steps provide value and which do not. Then remove those steps that do not provide value. The Lean Toolkit presented at the end of this book has a number of tools such as Value Stream Analysis or Non-Value Step Analysis that can help.

Example:

From:

| Fill Out and Submit Software Request Form | → | Validate Software Request Form | → | Approve Software Request | → | Notify User Of Software Request Status | → | Provide User With Instructions To Download Software | → | Download Software To User Device | → | Configure Software On User Device | → | Bill User For Software Requested |

To:

Remove This Step

| Fill Out and Submit Software Request Form | → | Validate Software Request Form | → | Approve Software Request | → | Notify User Of Software Request Status | → | Provide User With Instructions To Download Software | → | Download Software To User Device | → | Configure Software On User Device | → | Bill User For Software Requested |

With the above, the "Notify User Of Software Request Status" might be considered an extra step as the notification is already given when the user instructions are given in the next step.

Strategy #2 – Combine Or Consolidate Steps

For this strategy, some steps might be able to be combined into a single step.

From:

```
Fill Out and    →    Validate    →    Approve    →    Provide    →    Download    →    Configure    →    Bill User For
Submit               Software         Software         User With        Software To      Software         Software
Software             Request          Request          Instructions     User Device      On User          Requested
Request              Form                              To                                Device
Form                                                   Download
                                                       Software
```

To:

```
                                                          ┌─────────────────────────────┐
                                                          │ Package and automate         │
                                                          │ software download to install │
                                                          │ and configure on user device │
Fill Out and    →    Validate    →    Approve    →    Provide    →  │ Download    →    Configure │  →    Bill User For
Submit               Software         Software         User With     │ Software To      Software  │        Software
Software             Request          Request          Instructions  │ User Device      On User   │        Requested
Request              Form                              To            │                  Device    │
Form                                                   Download       └─────────────────────────────┘
                                                       Software
```

Here it has been determined that activities to download software can be automated such that the download and configuration steps can be done in a single step.

Strategy #3 – Move Steps That Cause Delays Into The Background

For this strategy, take steps that are non-value and cause delays and move them into the background such that they execute in parallel and have removed delays from the user.

From:

```
Fill Out and       Validate         Approve         Provide User       Download and      Bill User For
Submit             Software    →    Software   →    With          →    Configure    →    Software
Software     →     Request          Request         Instructions       Software To        Requested
Request            Form                             To Download        User Device
Form                                                Software
```

To:

```
Fill Out and       Validate          Provide User      Download and      Bill User For
Submit             Software          With         →    Configure    →    Software
Software     →     Request      →    Instructions      Software To        Requested
Request            Form              To Download       User Device
Form                                 Software
                    ↓
               Approve           Grant user software right away and get approvals in the background
               Software          ──────────────────────────────────────────────────────────→
               Request           If user not authorized, then remove the user's access to the software
```

In this example, getting management approval for software access can introduce days or even weeks of delays. Here, access to the software is automatically granted. If it is determined at a later time that the user shouldn't get the software, then their access is taken away.

Strategy #4 – Make Step Activities Move Faster (Increase Their Velocity)

With this strategy, you are not really taking anything out, but you are introducing automation, batching or other mechanisms to operate the step much faster.

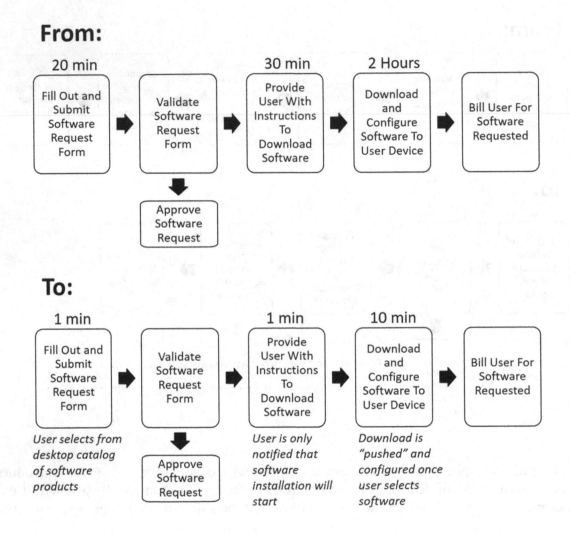

With the above, a strategy has been employed to utilize an automated software catalog. The user selects the desired software from the catalog. Once selected, the software will download and configure the software to the user's device.

Chapter

4

Agile Principles Applied To ITSM

Overview Of Agile

IT, for decades, has employed a development lifecycle for building IT solutions known as the Waterfall Development Model. Behold this in all its glory:

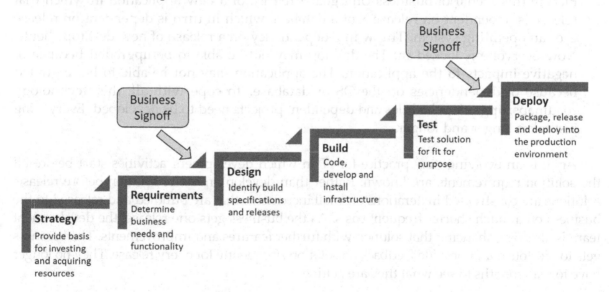

While this model has served IT well, it presents several problems in today's fast moving business climate. It's problematic for the following reasons:

It promotes distrust and bad relationships with the business.

The Business is skittish to sign off because they won't see anything else until the next release cycle. To cope with this, the business slows down IT by making sure every requirement they absolutely need is included. This is because they know there is a long period of time until they get to influence the solution again.

It's slow and highly wasteful.

There is a long gap between when the business signs off on the solution and when it is ready to go live. In fast moving business climate, there is a good chance that business conditions may have changed such that the original requirements may no longer be valid or are now incomplete. The business again slows down IT from releasing the solution because requirements have changed. Now IT has rework to do because some requirements have changed.

It's risk prone.

The business essentially walks away between the time they have signed off on requirements and when they come back for user acceptance and sign off. IT is essentially throwing the dice that they implemented everything the business needed. That they didn't misinterpret what they thought the business wanted. That the solution will be understood and usable by business stakeholders. That the solution can be operated day-to-day at acceptable cost and risk. When expectations are missed, it leads to either significant delays and costs or scrapping the effort altogether losing their entire investment in the solution.

It introduces a deadly cycle of complex big-bang releases and technology roadmaps.

Picture this scenario: Business Unit gets a release of a new application in which that release is dependent on release X of a database which in turn is dependent on release Y of an operating system. Throw in a dependency on a release of new desktop clients. Now everyone is locked in. The desktop may not be able to be upgraded because of negative impacts to the application. The application may not be able to be upgraded because of dependencies on the OS or database. To cope with all; this, technology roadmaps, upgrade schedules and dependent projects need to be developed. Everything just takes longer and longer.

Agile is an evolving new practice for IT in which development activities start before all the solution requirements are known. Rather than develop an entire solution before release, solutions are constructed in iterations of small increments that are bundled and released to the business on a much shorter frequent basis. As the business gets one release, the development team is already enhancing that solution with further features and improvements. The business gets to see, touch and provide feedback on solutions frequently for every release. They no longer have to wait months to see what they are getting.

Here is a living example from an actual large bank. The bank's lending division was overhauling their business intelligence reporting with all new reports, dashboards and analytics. The bank chose to use an agile approach to develop their solution. Development activities looked as follows:

1. Development teams met with bank lending representatives to identify data requirements and mocked up a small set of reports
2. The development team looked at the tasks they needed to do and created a backlog of work upon which they would prioritize and execute
3. This backlog was quickly chunked into "sprints" which represented short small releases that could be accomplished by the team

4. A first "sprint" release of the data model and subset of the reports was produced in 2 weeks

5. The representatives were called in to view the reports and provide feedback

6. Feedback was provided again by representatives directly to the development team

7. This added to the backlog and enhancements were added for the next "sprint" which was released 2 weeks later

8. Steps 5, 6 and 7 were then repeated about 3-4 more times until the backlog was greatly reduced and eventually completed

So what was the end result? Business representatives saw a working solution in just 2 weeks. Expectations were set such that they knew not everything would be included in the first release. They got to provide input all along the way. Satisfaction was high. Delivery was quick.

What would have happened if a Waterfall approach had been taken? Most likely weeks and weeks of user interviews and requirements gathering. Anxiety over signing off on a horde of requirements. Months of development activity for all those requirements. Missed expectations for reports that looked different than what they had expected them to be. Months go by. No value is delivered. How do we know that could happen? It actually did – with another development vendor prior to redoing the effort with the agile approach previously described.

Agile Concepts

So what does it mean to be agile when developing solutions?

Agile development is a means and set of solution development principles in which requirements and solutions evolve through team collaboration, adaptive planning, early customer feedback and continuous improvement. The key difference with Agile from past development practices is that the end state solution is not fully known at the time you start building and deploying. Rather than hold back build efforts until all requirements and design are complete, you start with an early set of requirements, build on those, get customer feedback, then update your requirements, build some more and so on until the full end state solution is reached.

Agile practices are not new. Their roots go back to the mid-1980s although incremental development methods themselves go back as far as the late 1950s. Over concerns about software development being too cumbersome and slow, a Manifesto for Agile Software Development was developed by the DSDM (Dynamic Systems Development Method) during the late 1990s and formally proclaimed in 2001. The Manifesto railed against highly regulated and regimented Waterfall methods and advocated a return to more lightweight and rapid development approaches. It's goal; was to promote better ways of developing software and valued customers, people, collaboration and rapid change over traditional documentation, contract negotiation, and following a strict plan.

A number of agile methods existed prior to publication of the Manifesto. These included practices such as DSDM XP, and Scrum developed during the 1990s.

Some of the key concepts of agile present interesting ways of working that are different than IT may be used to working with:
- Requirements are not fully known before you start building – they evolve over a continuous loop of customer interaction with the solution and feedback
- Customer interaction with the software as it is being constructed provides much more accurate requirements and greatly increases customer confidence in the solution than using interviews, documenting requirements in a presentation and asking for customer signoff
- Demonstrating working software to customers goes much farther than just presenting documents in a meeting
- Requirements are elaborated as Features and User Stories and closely tracked by Teams typically using Kanban Boards or other similar approaches and displayed publicly
- Daily "stand-up" meetings (also known as the daily scrum) are held to report progress toward the sprint goal, what will be done that day, and any roadblocks that might exist.
- Continuous development is promoted with a sharp focus on rapid response to change

Agile development methods break solutions down into small increments (Sometimes called Features and User Stories). These increments are then assigned to Iterations (short time frames called Sprints) that typically last from one to four weeks. Each iteration involves a cross-functional team working on all functions from planning to test. At the end of the iteration or Sprint, a working product is demonstrated to stakeholders. This greatly reduces risk and allows the project to adapt to changes quickly. An iteration does not produce a fully complete solution, but has enough functionality to be released to the customer. Multiple iterations might be required to fully release a product or new features. The Agile Operating Model presented later in this chapter shows a general approach that can be adopted by IT organizations.

An Agile Operating Model For ITSM

This section presents an overall operating model that can be used to build and develop services and products in the context of IT Service Management. In IT organizations, development of solutions doesn't start and end with applications. It includes those applications in an eco-sphere that is surrounded by supporting infrastructure, operations, Service Desk and other support functions. Release of an application by itself is problematic if these latter functions are not configured to operate the application at acceptable cost and risks to the business.

As a result, many projects will include not just the application development team, but also operational teams. Operating High Velocity ITSM includes the use of DevOps. Therefore the implication is that solutions under development will always have at a minimum, two teams: Development and Operations.

The model presents a way for how multiple teams may extend an agile development approach to accommodate use of multiple teams. Essentially this is having each team individually follow agile practices and working in Sprints. The team Sprints themselves are aligned and coordinated across all teams into a planned Release. This sometimes has been referred to as "Scrum of Scrums" in terms of its approach.

The model is presented as follows:

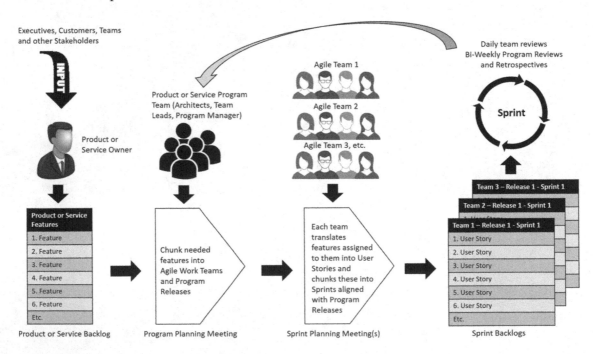

Let's follow the model above in counter-clockwise fashion starting at the upper left:

A service (or product) starts with Service Strategy. Executives, meet with customers and other stakeholders to determine what is needed. From this, they determine a service or product position and what key business outcomes they will be investing in.

A Service Owner (or Product Owner) is then assigned. This role reviews the strategy and creates a vision of the service. Key features are identified and inventoried. This inventory becomes the Service (or Product) Backlog.

At this point, a Service Team is pulled together. This team consists of an overall Program Manager, Architects and Team Leads. Note that many services are usually dependent on other supporting services to operate. As an example, an Email Service depends on supporting services like Network Management, Server Management, etc. Therefore, the Program Team will bring in a Team Lead person from each dependent service as well as a Team Lead for the Service being constructed. Once pulled together, a Program Planning Meeting is established to:

1) Take the features in the Backlog and assign them to the Team Leads who will own them
2) Assign each Feature to a Program Release (e.g. Features 1-4 will be in Release 1, Features 5-7 in Release 2, etc.)

Now each Team Lead assembles their Agile Team and holds a Sprint Planning Meeting. The goals of the Sprint Planning Meeting are to:

1) Translate the Features assigned to them into User Stories (Tasks that the team will accomplish but described slightly differently
2) Assign each User Story to a Release Sprint looking at which Features were assigned to which Releases
3) Coordinate which User Stories will be completed in each Sprint and Release with all the other Agile Teams to ensure that each Release will include a unified and cohesive set of deployable Features (e.g. if Feature 1, for example, requires a server upgrade, then the Agile Team handling the Servers will ensure that the Upgrade User Story will be in place at the same point that Feature 1 is released).
4) Finalize the Sprint Backlog (Inventory of User Stories to be completed for the Sprint)

Now Sprint 1 – Release 1 starts. For this, each Agile Team is working on their User Stories planned for that Sprint. Each Team holds daily (and brief) meetings to discuss progress on the previous day's User Stories, handle any blockers to team efforts, and determine what will be accomplished for the next day. The Team Lead coordinates any blockers or other issues with the other Team Leads as necessary.

As the Sprint completes, the Program Team meets to review all the User Stories and Features originally planned for the Release. If all looks good, then the Sprint is considered complete and goes off for Continuous Release (described later in this book). Features are validated for the next release and off everyone goes again.

More formal methods are available in the industry that address use of Agile for larger projects and multiple teams. Examples of these include:

- Scaled Agile Framework (SAFe)

- Disciplined Agile Delivery (DAD)
- Large-scale scrum (LeSS)
- Nexus (scaled professional Scrum)
- Scrum at Scale
- Enterprise Scrum
- Setchu (Scrum-based lightweight framework)
- Xscale

Infrastructure Projects Can Also Be Agile

There is a misconception that agile development approaches can only be used for application development projects. That it doesn't apply for infrastructure projects. In actuality, almost any development or infrastructure effort can be done as an agile project. It still comes down to the Features and User Stories that get built and deciding which Sprint those features and User Stories will reside in.

Let's look at an example of how this might be done. The desire here is to implement a new Asset Management solution. Needed here is a new tool, new processes, operating roles and responsibilities and an effort to migrate current asset data to the new system.

Here is how the Sprints for such an effort might be laid out:

Sprint	Scope
01	Install out of box hardware and setup network connections including connection to the cloud provider
02	Install out of box tool and databases
03	Install screens with empty fields - no data shown and demo these with user representatives to make sure all needed data elements are in the solution
04	Install workflows between the screens and use these to walk through use cases going from screen to screen and confirming the data fields on each screen
05	Build and install asset dashboards reports displaying only the columns and headers (not any data) - demo these with user representatives to make sure all needed dashboard and report data elements are in the solution

Sprint	Scope
06	Install a small sample of asset data and use this to populate the screens, dashboards and reports built previously - demo these with user representatives to reaffirm that all needed dashboard and report data elements are in the solution
07	Import user security groups, profiles and logins and test to make sure they access right screens, reports and fields – conduct a use case walk-through again, this time by asset management operating role to make sure each role has the proper access and authority rights.
08	Install monitoring and log tools that will be used to capture changes in asset management operating state
09	Install and test notifications, emails, logs and alerts (e.g. generate an alert each time asset information has been modified)
10	Extract and import existing production data into the solution as a test run for deployment – this includes capabilities to bulk load assets
11	Build asset export features and test these to see if assets can be downloaded to other venues such as a text file or spreadsheet
12	Build out any custom queries for searching and finding assets – again execute with use cases to help drive what kinds of queries should be built and made public to users
13	Install support infrastructure such as service desk support categories and linkage to service desk tools to support new solution
14	Reserve this Sprint for training users and support staff for the new asset management solution
15	Reserve this Sprint for deployment and operational readiness activities – then deploy the solution out to production

Notice the agility being employed here versus a typical infrastructure Waterfall Project. Assuming each Sprint is about 1 week long, business users are brought in as early as Week 3 to start seeing a working solution instead of waiting months and months before they see anything. The solution is constructed in small increments which focuses implementation teams. Management can see progress by looking at progress within each Sprint.

The point here is that anything can go agile. You just simply identify your solution backlog and then chunk it out into sprints. No need to treat infrastructure projects any differently than application development projects.

Maintenance and Support Can Be Agile

IT Service Management is not just about building and managing IT services, it also includes the ongoing daily support for handling incidents, problems, application management, and patching of hardware and software. Since these are not really building and developing, can they be handled with agile approaches?

The answer is yes. Here is how one large government agency took on this task:

1) Incidents, problems, bugs and patches were classified into the services that were impacted

2) Support teams were assigned to "own" each incident, problem, bug or patch

3) Tasks to fix software and hardware issues were placed and managed on a separate Kanban Board for each team

4) Each team organized their assigned tasks into Sprints – meaning they were grouped into what Sprint they would be fixed in

5) Sprints were only 1 week in duration

6) Larger tasks were broken down into sub-tasks if the teams determined that the main task could not be accomplished in a single Sprint

7) Daily standup meetings were held with each team to track progress

Prior to using the above approach, the support teams were inundated with hundreds of bugs, patches and requests for a new service that had just been deployed. Support and technical teams were overwhelmed with the backlog and struggled to prioritize and find a way to effectively deal with all the work. Users of the service were extremely frustrated and questioned whether it should have rolled out in the first place.

Once the Agile approach was introduced, things moved fast. Batching tasks into Sprints allowed for more work to be completed faster. Users saw the progress on a Sprint by Sprint basis and their confidence in the solution increased. The backlog of hundreds of items rapidly decreased week by week until only a dozen or so items were left after a 6 month period.

Chapter 5

DevOps Applied To ITSM

DevOps Overview

Does your IT operational organization can go into chaos when new IT solutions are deployed? Doe the IT organization experience untold amounts of unplanned labor, cost overruns, delays and service outages each time a new solution goes live into production?

The most costly, resource intensive and time consuming events occur when new solutions go live. This is an expensive problem that has been around IT for decades. Root cause? Lack of integration, communication and partnership between IT development and operations organizations. Historically, development teams finish their piece, then throw it over the wall to operations to deploy and operate. Operations staff then scramble to understand what needs to be deployed and supported. They also discover many operational elements that were not planned for creating more delays. Other missing items get "discovered" when users call issues in to the Service Desk.

You can also throw competing objectives into the mix between these two organizations. Development teams want to get code done fast, submit it on time and move onto the next exciting project. Development is done when the solution is deployed. Operations wants to ensure incidents, problems and unplanned issues do not occur in production. Operations is never done as they have to manage the solution on an ongoing basis day-to-day. Development embraces change. Operations embraces not changing.

The goal of DevOps is to get these two organizations together. Not only get them together, but make sure each side communicates, operates effectively and efficiently and removes wasteful activities that result in delays and unnecessary costs. In other words, go live with a service, not chunks of application code that then need to be operated and supported. For this reason, the practice of DevOps includes a strong focus on agile development practices and embedding a culture of cooperation between the two types of teams. If the business only sees IT value at the point a service is delivered, and value is not seen unless both utility (function) and warranty (service is there when needed) are in place, does it not make sense to build both sides of the solution together?

So what is DevOps about? It is a culture and practice that emphasizes the collaboration of software developers and IT Operations to allow for rapid and frequent build, test, and release of reliable software. It includes:

- Integrated teams (Development, Operations and the Business)
- Continuous releases and deployments
- Continuous testing
- Automation for velocity
- Operations involvement at the front end
- Agile practices to deliver in small increments

Some key areas of focus for IT operations to successfully work with Development organizations include the following:

Engage through service offerings that Development can easily consume.
Come to the Development table with a catalog of service offerings – not thousands of questions. Services should exist to handle hosting, monitoring, deployment, handling incidents, problems and requests. Stop trying to build support over and over for each development project.

Instill Agile and Lean into Service Management processes.
There is typically lots of delays and waste in Service Management processes. Things that could be done much more efficiently. This book addresses this throughout in earlier chapters covering Lean IT and later chapters on leaning out ITSM processes. Keep a sharp and aggressive eye out for tasks that provide little value. Eliminate or change tasks that create delays or hold things up.

Engage early in the development lifecycle.
Be part of the entire development lifecycle process, from strategy to design to build, test and deploy. Don't just come in at the end or wait for development teams to get to their deployment stage before you start. This causes slowdowns and delays. Go live together. The Operational Readiness Framework described later in this chapter describes how you might accomplish this.

Aggressively automate repeatable tasks.
Be aggressive at automation. Be aggressive with self-service. Identify pockets of tasks that operations staff does manually over and over. Is there a way to accomplish those things much faster?

Dev and Ops both need to be agile and deliver in a continuous manner.
In the Agile chapter of this book is a discussion on emerging practices around continuous release, continuous testing and continuous deployment. These hold a lot of promise for freeing development to deploy releases at almost any point safely. Gone are the need for major release upgrades or extensive coordination for technology roadmaps and upgrades.

A DevOps Success Story

Here is a live case example from a large food distribution company of what value occurs when you integrate development and operations teams from the start:

The company had invested over $100M to overhaul food operations at each of their sites. The development team was stalled for almost 3 months arguing over whether a fat or thin client should be used at each distribution site. Each side fought over the merits, the pros and cons, the technical advantages or disadvantages without coming to a conclusion.

In walks a representative from the operations staff. Not part of all the previous arguments, the representative simply asked "what happens when the disk drive in the client goes down?". The initial reaction from the development team was to dismiss the representative. "That's operational stuff! We're in design mode right now. Come back when we're ready to deploy." Insistent, the representative walked them through an interesting scenario. "When the disk fails, a repair person will be dispatched to the site. They will replace the drive, wire it back up, close the machine bay door and leave. Is that acceptable if you have a fat client? Are there not recovery scripts to run, restore activities for the database?" "So what?" was the response from the development team. "The repair person then has to run the recovery scripts".

"Not so fast said the representative". "Repair people don't come with those skills".

"Then have 2 people come out to the site", said the development team.

"That's very complicated to coordinate – and expensive" replied the representative. "How quickly do you need the machine to be back in operating state?"

"4 hours", said the Development team.

"You realize that most repair vendors charge a premium to meet a repair target like that. The costs for all that will be expensive".

A discussion around the costs then took place. This company had over 24,000 remote sites around the country. It was easily seen that the ongoing annual costs to maintain and repair fat clients at remote sites was going to cost more on an annual basis than the entire cost of the project. Now the Development team was worried.

"What happens if we have a thin client at each site?" they asked.

"Then the repair person quickly comes in, fixes the drive and leaves – nothing more to be done!" was the answer. With this, the deadlock on fat versus thin client was quickly resolved (for financial – not technical reasons now) and the Development team was able to continue.

That's the kind of value that can happen when you get development and operations together.

Fusing Development and Operations Together

Developers think they understand operations but in reality have quite a limited view of what is involved. Operations doesn't really understand development and surprisingly, many support and technical staff don't operate with even a simple development lifecycle (design, build, test, deploy) when they implement their solutions. Operations typically acts in a "just get it done" mode.

Simply throwing these two organizations in a room together in the hopes that things will change is rife with disaster. Development needs to understand that putting operational components into place are part of their development activities. Operations needs to assist development in this task by asking the right questions at each stage of the development lifecycle and offering support solutions in the form of services.

Implementing applications is not enough for the business. That is only the utility side of the solution. The business wants the whole service. This means that you should be concerned not only for the applications and technologies being deployed, that is the utility aspects of the service, but also warranty requirements such as availability, capacity, support processes, trained support staff and the need to operate at acceptable cost and risk to the business. IT Development teams and operational support teams need to work together. The Operational Readiness Framework presented in this chapter outlines a suggested approach for doing so.

The Operational Readiness Framework

The Operational Readiness Framework ensures you select the appropriate solution operational support and helps to construct this as the application itself is being developed throughout the entire development lifecycle. This provides you with the prevention (or early warning in the worst case) of any possible cost overruns, project delays or exposure to service outages. It also shortens the development cycle in that both applications and IT support solutions are developed in tandem releasing together at production deployment time.

The framework provides you with a broad overview of support requirements that are needed for almost any application solution. You can (and should) modify it for any application unique support requirements that may not already exist in the framework. The solution support and delivery strategy enables you to review every support area in the framework to determine how it will be handled. This can consist from simply reusing pre-existing tools and support staff to buying or outsourcing support from third parties.

During the early stages of development for a new solution, use the framework to identify how each support area will be provided. As you go through each area, develop an appropriate support strategy for the solution. Can you reuse something already in place? Will you have to build something new? The table below provides examples of options that you might take for each support area in the framework:

Strategy	Description
Eliminate	The process area is not needed to support the solution being developed
Reuse	Reuse existing support tools, people or suppliers to support the solution with no more than minor modifications needed
Modify	Existing support tools, people or suppliers exist but changes will be needed to adequately support the solution (e.g. new technology upgrades, changes to support contracts, etc.)
Build	Support tools, people, or suppliers do not exist and the desired strategy is to build a support solution internally
Buy	Support tools, people or suppliers do not exist and the desired strategy is to buy these from external sources and manage them internally
Outsource	Support tools, people, or suppliers do not exist and the desired strategy is to outsource these areas to third parties
Cloud	Support tools and solutions will leverage Cloud or Software as a Service technologies.

As an example outcome of this analysis, the Strategy stage will identify a management strategy that:

- Builds skills in house for support of servers, application, network and storage
- Outsources monitoring and incident management to a 3rd party
- Establishes an in-house program for training end users and targets in-house process improvements to handle solution changes
- Implements a load balancing solution for availability
- Reuses existing capacity services and capabilities.

The design and transition stages will execute this strategy, ensuring that the planned elements are implemented in tandem with the application development effort.

The table below highlights operational readiness activities by ITSM lifecycle stage. If you have an application solution going live, walk down this table to identify how each element will be delivered.

The diagram below shows how the ITSM Service Lifecycle stages can be used as developmental phases for building the operational support.

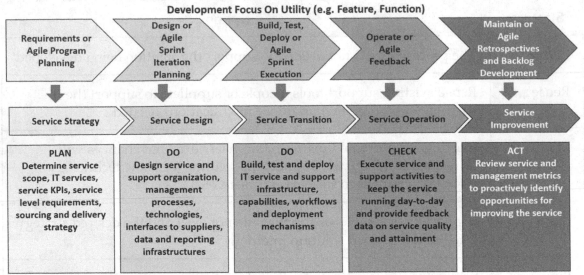

At the top, a typical development Waterfall lifecycle or Agile equivalent is shown and linked to each ITSM Lifecycle Stage. Those stages should be done in parallel with the application development efforts at the top. For example, when undertaking the application requirements or Agile Program Planning stage, Service Strategy activities should occur at the same time. The key point is that operational build activities start at the point the application development effort first starts - not at the end. Operations is involved with development at each stage. They deploy together as an integrated team. Not one after the other.

In an Agile development effort, it is not uncommon to have at least 2 Sprints operating at the same time. One Sprint would be devoted to development of features and user stories that build the functionality (or utility) part of the solution. Another Sprint would be devoted to building the operational features and user stories that provide ensure the service will be there when needed and can operate at acceptable costs and risks (warranty). Both Sprints would be coordinated via a Release Program. More on this in the Agile chapter of this book.

The large boxes under each ITSM Lifecycle Stagee summarize which operational activities should occur in that stage. For example, when you are in the Service Design Stage (in parallel with application design), you should undertake operational readiness activities to design the Service Support Organization, processes, technologies, data and reporting infrastructure.

The table below provides a set of considerations for each stage from an ITSM point of view, looking at both development and operations. These activities can be done parallel between IT application development teams and IT service management teams.

The tables below outline what operational items need to be understood, built and addressed at each lifecycle stage:

Strategy - Undertake this in parallel with application solution requirements building
In this stage we focus on high level service needs such as solution key requirements, sourcing strategy, availability needs and expected business volumes. Examples of things that may need to be considered in place for production can include:

- Service billing and chargeback to users
- Managing the impact of business volumes
- Managing the business relationship
- Updating the IT service portfolio
- Determining the ongoing solution support strategy which can include 3rd party suppliers as well as internal IT resources
- How to obtain resources to handle support functions

A checklist of items to be developed during this stage for Development and Operations includes:

Development Team Considerations	Operations Team Considerations
Overall Solution Model	High Level Service Requirements:
Business Volumes	- Performance
Specialized Support Needs	- Availability
Implementation Timeframes	- Incident Support
High Level Functional Requirements	Support and Delivery Strategy
Development Organization	Solution Operating Plan
Working Standards	Current Support Capabilities
Sourcing Partners	Hosting/Sourcing Partners
Application Architecture	Required Support Suppliers
Overall Enterprise Fit	Timeframes For Production
Standards To Be Used	Ongoing Operational Costs
Frameworks To Be Used	Management Tooling Architecture
Opportunities For Reuse	Support Skills Needs
Estimated Build Costs	

As part of a quality assurance review, check that these items are all in place:

- ✓ A support strategy for each item checklist item (as shown in the above table) for all the other lifecycle stages
- ✓ A solution management tooling architecture
- ✓ An operating plan for the solution
- ✓ An application service targets and requirements
- ✓ Forecasted application business volumes
- ✓ Documented results from any support capabilities (process, technology, organization or skills if these were done)
- ✓ A documented training strategy

✓ A high level solution support sourcing strategy
✓ Cost estimates and a cost model for building and operating the solution
✓ A documented high level deployment strategy
✓ A project plan for conducting design activities

Design - This should be done in parallel with application design or planning activities associated with an Agile Sprint

During this stage, we focus on design for each solution support area. Design tasks might include selection of specific tools, customizing tools, putting support contracts together, identifying event alarms and alerts, designing backup and recovery procedures or designing support processes. Examples of things that may need to be in place for production can include:

- Coordinating solution design efforts for support and operation
- Updating the service catalog for the solution
- Designing configurations to support service targets and agreements
- Designing solution availability and risk mitigation elements
- Designing and sizing capacity and performance
- Designing how the solution can recover from a major disaster
- Securing the solution from security threats
- Procuring, coordinating and managing suppliers

A checklist of items to be developed during this stage for Development and Operations includes:

Development Team Considerations	Operations Team Considerations
Application Designs	Operational Architecture
Software Package Customizations	Availability Designs
Testing Requirements	Capacity Designs
Capacity Requirements	Capacity Estimates
Component Configurations	Service Continuity Designs
Component Configurations	Security Designs
Procurement Requirements	Deployment Designs/Strategy
Operational Detailed Requirements:	Process and technology designs for each
- Required Alerts	support area in the framework
- Backup Requirements	Support Roles/Responsibilities
- Solution Configurations	Operational Control Tasks
Data Architecture	Facilities Designs
Functional Architecture	Monitoring Designs
Technical Architecture:	Procurement Requirements
- Application	Training Artifacts
- Middleware/Messaging	Management Technology Specifications
- Network	
- Transaction	
- Database	
-Models/Data Design	

As part of a quality assurance review, check that these items are all in place:

- ✓ A design package that provides detailed specifications for each framework item that is in scope
- ✓ Solution build and operating costs that have been reviewed with key solution stakeholders

Transition - Undertake in parallel with application build, test and deployment or during execution of Agile Iterations and Sprints

In this stage, we focus on build, test and deployment of the designed hardware, software and management processes for each solution support area. Transition tasks might include implementation of systems management tools, implementation of event monitors and agents, building and testing of server and desktop images, software distribution activities, and construction of physical data center facilities and closets. Examples of things that may need to be in place for production can include:

- Solution deployment activities such as packaging, configuring, imaging and software distribution
- Handling of solution changes and releases
- Handling of service assets and configurations
- Testing of the solution

A checklist of items to be developed during this stage for Development and Operations includes:

Development Team Considerations	Operations Team Considerations
Application Coding Package Implementation Migration/Code Libraries Rollout Schedules/Volumes Maintenance Needs Testing and Validation User Acceptance	Support Call Lists Release Deployment Configurations Server/Desktop Images Operational Testing Site Surveys/Preparation User/Support Training Process Implementation Operational Integration: Service Desk Technical Support Operation Control Facilities Management Application Management Production Cutover

As part of a quality assurance review, check that these items are all in place:

- ✓ Operational Scripts
- ✓ Job Schedules
- ✓ Run Books
- ✓ Solution Documentation that is stored in knowledge base
- ✓ Configured and installed security
- ✓ Access IDs and Passwords
- ✓ Solution Components that are configured for production
- ✓ Accepted Operational Test Results
- ✓ Users that have been trained to use the application
- ✓ Solution Known Errors that have been given to the Service Desk
- ✓ Monitoring Agents for production use
- ✓ Documented Support Processes
- ✓ Support Staff resources assigned for each needed operating role
- ✓ Service management tools
- ✓ Physical sites that are environmentally ready to accept solution components
- ✓ Application components in a staging area ready for deployment
- ✓ Third party agreements are in place for supporting the solution
- ✓ Accepted User Acceptance Results
- ✓ Updated Solution operating costs that have been reviewed with stakeholders
- ✓ An operating risk assessment that has been accepted by IT and business stakeholders
- ✓ Detailed Transition Plans

Operation - Do this in parallel with application early life support and then keep this ongoing At this point, your solution should already be operating in production. Tasks in this phase represent ongoing activities to deliver services provided by the application solution. These activities focus on meeting service targets, delivering the services, monitoring them, processing incidents, problems and changes, maintaining applications and providing operational data. Examples of things that may need to be in place for production can include:

- Handling of incidents
- Handling of problems
- Solution monitoring
- Managing access with control lists, groups, policies, user IDs and passwords
- Handling of solution requests
- Updating Service Desk call scripts, support models, and ticket classifications
- Service Desk agent training and skills readiness
- Service Desk contacts for incidents and requests
- Enforcement of license policies
- Backup/Restore management of solution data and applications
- Job event and schedule management
- Service startup and shutdown coordination controls
- Transfer of files with controlled delivery of data to business partners

- Handling of media artifacts
- Command Center consoles and operator views
- Transaction queue handling with middleware controls
- Print operations
- Management of spare parts inventories and dispatch
- Hardware, software and network maintenance activities
- Desktop Support management for PCs, laptops and other devices
- Dispatching hands-on repair as needed
- Management of log files and application queues
- Solution monitoring and forwarding of events
- Run book documentation and other knowledge to operate and support the solution
- Build out of physical processing sites
- Managing power, floor space, and server center environmental controls
- Managing physical site security, access badges and security cameras
- Training for IT support staff

A checklist of items to be developed during this stage for Development and Operations includes:

Development Team Considerations	Operations Team Considerations

None - at this point the Application Management should take over for ongoing application maintenance and support.	These are considerations by ongoing operational delivery teams:
	   - Delivering Services
	   - Ongoing Support
	   - Monitoring/Event Management
	   - Maintenance of applications
	   - Maintenance of IT infrastructure
	   - Execution of operational control tasks
	      - Incident,/Problem Management
	      - Request Fulfillment
	      - Access Management

As part of a quality assurance review, check that these items are all in place:

✓ Management approvals to proceed with cutover activities
✓ A back out/recovery plan in case of any deployment failures
✓ Solution operating costs reviewed with key solution stakeholders
✓ All components should be ready to go live

Improvement - Undertake this in parallel with ongoing application management activities or during Agile retrospectives and planning sessions

This effort runs in parallel as a service is in the Operations Stage. Focus on reporting service quality and proactively reviewing the solution to identify ongoing improvements. Examples of things that may need to be in place for production can include:

- Solution service metrics and reporting
- Managing feedback on service performance and quality
- Ongoing reviews of solution quality
- Regular reviews of feedback and planning for the next release or Sprint

A checklist of items to be developed during this stage for Development and Operations includes:

Development Team Considerations	Operations Team Considerations
None – at this point the Application Management function should takes over for ongoing application improvement.	Collecting Service Measurements Service Quality Reporting Review Of Service And Operational Results To Identify Further Opportunities For Improvements.

The considerations presented here should better focus application and operations teams so that they work together towards a solution, deploy that solution and avoid the chaos that can occur each time a major new service goes into production.

As part of a quality assurance review, check that these items are all in place:

✓ Confirm that operational support activities are working successfully with minimal issues
✓ A service improvement plan is in place or additional improvement items are being added to the Agile Product Backlog
✓ Ongoing operating costs that stay within forecasted levels
✓ Solution benefits that are being achieved
✓ User satisfaction with the service

Bundling Operational Services For Solutions

As can be seen in the proceeding section, there are lots of operational support services that underpin application solutions for the business. When you take into account support services like the Service Desk, incident, problem, request management, monitoring and many others, the list gets a bit large. From the Servicing ITSM book that describes all these services in detail there are about 50-55 of them.

Rather than overwhelm development teams and business users with all these, it makes better sense to bundle and package these into generalized operations and support services that would be more easily consumable. The suggested approach is to adopt what the industry has been evolving to in the Cloud Services market. Many vendors there have been offering their services along the lines of Platform-As-A-Service or Infrastructure-As-A-Service offerings. With these, each bundle provides a host of management features. Infrastructure-As-A-Service, for example, might include Service Desk support, Incident Management, Request Fulfillment for infrastructure items and availability monitoring. The user does not have to ask for these separately.

The strategy here for ITSM is to create bundles like these internally that can be offered to development teams. With this, the discussion around solution operational needs can start with the service being offered and proceed from there. This is much quicker and efficient than trying to re-architect operational solutions from the ground up each time a new application is being developed. If the solution needs Service Desk and Incident support, then a service already exists to do those functions. It's just a matter of onboarding the new application to that service.

Development team interaction with Operations then becomes simpler. Developers can pick and choose through the Operations Service Catalog for the services they need. Operations then on boards those solutions so they can be subscribed to those services. Any unique needs that may be missing then fall into one of the 7 strategies described earlier. Do we say no? Buy it somewhere else? Add it to the service portfolio?

A suggested model for support bundles that can be offered to Developers is that as shown below:

With this model, operational support services are bundled into the service offerings shown above (e.g. Basic Support Service, Infrastructure As Service, etc. The service offerings are stacked. Developers may consume starting at the bottom and then add additional offerings as they need them.

The principles around how these services are offered is as follows:

- **The Basic Support Service is required to use any other service.** This service is offered at a fixed monthly and/or per seat rate to cover basic infrastructure needs such as the Service Desk, network, physical infrastructure to house equipment and basic monitoring to indicate whether the hardware itself is up and running. An option for this service (at an additional cost) can include the ability for development teams to place their own hardware into the data center. With this, they get the ability to house the hardware, but they have to maintain everything else on their own. Some enterprising IT organizations actually offer something like this as a way of renting out unused Data Center facilities or turning unused physical infrastructure into profitable cash flow.

- **Infrastructure As Service Offering manages base operating system software and related items.** With this, development teams can have all the low level hardware and systems software configured and managed for them. They are still responsible for applications and databases. This offering requires the Basic Support Service as a pre-requisite.

- **Platform As Service provides support for specific platforms such as database systems, SharePoint or GIS infrastructure.** These are items that are not complete applications in themselves, but are provided as platforms to development staff for their use. Development teams write code against these platforms via database or API calls. Both the Basic Support Service and Infrastructure As Service offerings are pre-requisites to use this service. Developers still manage their own applications.

- **Application As Service provides the full end-to-end support from the hardware up through the application.** With this offerings, operations will not only manage the underlying infrastructure, but also the applications that use that infrastructure. Once built, developers then hand off the full solution to operations. Operations will perform Application Management functions to maintain and operate the applications end to end. This offering requires the Basic Support Service, Infrastructure As Service, and Platform As Service offerings as pre-requisites.

- **Value Add-On Services provide management of specific components such as storage, desktop, printing and mobile devices.** Developers may select any of these services as they need to. Only the Basic Support Service is required as a pre-requisite.

Use of bundled service offerings such as those described above makes working with development teams much easier. The conversation turns from "what is it you need?" to "here is what we have to offer".

Operations Support For Development Teams

Developers are customers too. Towards that end, Operations could offer services that help development teams with their efforts. Development staff prefers to work on coding and testing. Not on setting up development environments, developer workstations or other temporary infrastructure.

The diagram below presents a set of operational services that could be provided to development staff to help them with their efforts and make them more productive.

Hosting	Operational Readiness Consulting	Development Environment Support	Sandbox and Demo Support	Release Operations	Test Support	Developer Workstation Support
Package IT Support Services So That They Plug and Play Into Applications Being Developed (e.g. Monitoring, Request Fulfillment, Incident Handling, Patch Management, etc.	Planning and consulting support to ensure solution being developed can operate day-to-day at acceptable cost and risk	Operations Support for the development environment (e.g. (backup, recovery, monitoring, archiving, availability solution hardware and network sizing, etc.)	Support that quickly provisions and decommissions sandboxes and demos	Code management and migration to Test, QA and Production environments	Spin up and tear down of test environments, testing support and test data creation and management	Workstation procurement, provisioning and configuration

we don't having to take physical network outages or ... ...
to maximize use of storage. Hardware can fail and if so, the failure ... ...
... ... to ... copies or ... by relocating the ... ...
... ... from the data center itself.

How Virtualization Works

Examples of virtualization functions are many but all involve reducing the ... ...
... ...

Chapter

6

Virtualization Applied To ITSM

Virtualization Overview

Virtualization is about separating configuration items such as servers, storage, PCs, networks, applications, operating systems and even data centers themselves from their physical components. The goal is to maximize use of hardware resources by recreating multiple logical versions of those resources. For example, a physical server might host multiple virtual servers.

Consumers of virtualized configuration items are unaware that those items have been virtualized. In the case of servers, for example, the server acts as if it were a physical device even though it is not. Some of the key benefits of using virtualization include:

- Maximizing use of physical infrastructure components (e.g. rather than purchase 4 physical servers that run at 20% utilized, purchase 1 physical server that hosts 4 virtual servers)

- Quick recovery of components if they fail (e.g. failure of a virtualized server can quickly be restored electronically by stopping and restarting that virtualized server)

- Capability to quickly provision components in minutes versus delays and overhead to procure, install and configure physical versions of those components

- Capability to quickly move components from one physical platform to another to balance demand (e.g. move a highly utilized server to another physical host or offload servers to a physical host that is less utilized

- In some cases achieve economies of scale in licensing costs.

Initially starting with virtualization of servers, technologies have been rapidly evolving to virtualize almost anything physical that resides in the data center. Network devices can be virtualized such that those devices can be configured, quickly restored and maintained without having to take physical network components down. Storage can be virtualized to maximize use of storage hardware and quickly provision or decommission storage. Desktops can be virtualized to gain benefits of easier image management, efficient patching and upgrades and quick recovery from hardware failures.

How Virtualization Works

In concept, virtualization has many benefits, but an understanding of the mechanics of virtualization is important to avoid problems. The diagram below illustrates an example for hosting servers:

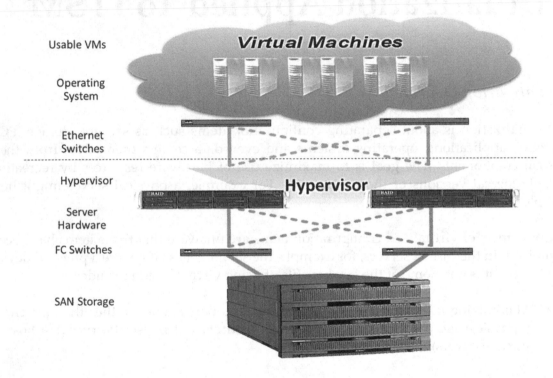

As shown above, virtual servers are connected through the network to a hosting platform called a Hypervisor. The Hypervisor plays a critical role in making virtual servers look like real physical servers. It is basically a combination of physical operating system hardware and software that creates, moves, and swaps virtual machines in and out. It utilizes complex scheduling and interrupt mechanisms to make decisions on how to best utilize the physical hardware. For example, a virtual machine that is idle and waiting on something may get swapped out for another virtual machine that is ready to process something.

As a virtual machine is swapped out, all of the operating elements are carefully stored in a swap area. This includes the operating system, any applications currently running, the contents of anything stored in memory and input/output buffers. When swapped in, those elements are all restored back to the physical host device. Priority mechanisms help determine which virtual machines may be prioritized for swap in or swap out.

An understanding of this is key to determining which workloads work best with virtualization and which may not. A virtual machine that has heavy I/O processing may not be as good a fit as heavy I/O demands may monopolize swap in and out resources and overload the Hypervisor. Likewise, a workload that has intense processing needs may lighten the load on the Hypervisor but over-consume the physical host processors. Workloads that have fairly even balances between processing and I/O may have the best fit with virtualization solutions. Management and support of the Hypervisor will have to monitor use of physical resources and attempt to re-balance them as usage demand changes.

Virtualization and Change Management

Virtualization and automation technologies go a tremendous way towards speeding up ITSM Service Transition activities but they carry a double-edge sword when it comes to risk.

When changes and releases are implemented onto virtualized hardware, the risk goes way down. Since software is controlling the activities – not human hands – mistakes are less likely to be made. The implementation will proceed the way it was programmed to do. Therefore use of these technologies will actually serve to reduce risk when transitioning solutions to the live environment. As long as it is a virtualized device being changed, changes may easily be backed out. A more severe error can be quickly recovered by re-provisioning the device.

The opposite holds true if you are changing, not the virtualized devices, but the Hypervisors and Bare Metal configurations that the virtual devices run on. Since the simplest change to these elements could impact many devices all at once, the risk goes way up – even for the smallest kinds of changes.

The same risk situation holds true for automation scripts and programs. These do wonderful things in the way of efficiency, enforcing standards and preserving accuracy. Unfortunately, changes to those elements present elevated levels of risk. An error in an automated script could result in prorogation of operating, data and processing issues very quickly throughout the IT infrastructure. Incidents and problems will be initially hard to trace back to the script being at fault versus the applications or infrastructure that failed.

The bottom line is that you need to be aware of a perverse difference from historical thinking around change management when it comes to virtualization. Large changes to virtualized devices can occur at lower levels of risk. Small simple changes to Hypervisors and Bare Metal configuration items could pose high risks.

Chapter 7

Integrated ALM Applied To ITSM

Overview Of ALM

It would be foolish in today's world to propose buying and installing one tool to handle service incidents, another to handle service requests, another to handle service changes, another to build and manage a service catalog. The work across all these functions needs to be integrated and for years now, tool vendors have provided us with ITSM suites of tools that integrate these functions together.

The development world has similar issues. Requirements need to be generated. Application code needs to be tied back to those requirements. Version management of code needs to happen. Code needs to be pushed into releases, compiled, tested and deployed. Projects that do all this need to be managed. Yet, historically, these functions have happened with a wide set of different separate tools with little integration between them. What is needed, is an integrated suite of tools and workflows that handle many of the functions needed for developers. Integrated Application Lifecycle Management (ALM) is a modern push to do just that.

As ITSM processes and tools integrate and automate many of the operations and service management functions, ALM tools integrate and automate many of the functions needed for application development. With ALM, development tools, users and information is synchronized and linked together throughout the application development stages. The goal is to speed up development tasks, avoid errors, enforce working standards and ensure free and flowing communication exists throughout all the development teams.

IT Service Management provides a comprehensive framework for building and managing an entire service delivered to the business. Integrated ALM provides a comprehensive approach for development of applications which underpin that service. It's not a far stretch to expect that ALM will extend itself into the DevOps world in the near future.

The ALM Operating Model

ALM starts with the Software Development Lifecycle (SDLC) and provides a broader perspective that adds in disciplines like DevOps, Continuous Testing, Continuous Release and others. It also includes ongoing management of application software which is essentially the ITSM Application Management function.

The diagram below summarizes ALM:

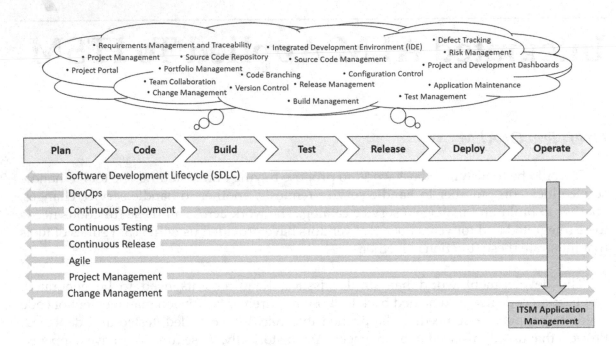

In the above, the items in the Cloud part of the picture represent tooling functions. In an Integrated ALM world, these tools are integrated and pass a consistent set of information between them. The tooling functions in their entirety support the ALM stages for planning, coding, building, testing, releasing, deploying and operating. The ALM stages operate with modern IT methods such as Agile, DevOps, etc. Ongoing management of applications leverages the ITSM Applications Management function to maintain and manage applications until they are retired.

Chapter
8

Cloud Computing Impact On ITSM

Cloud Computing Overview

One of the best and leading disruptive technology advances in IT is Cloud Computing. This is really a service delivery channel. It provides hosting services using the internet in the form of on-demand access to a pool of computing resources such as servers, storage, applications and networks. Some of the key benefits include:

- The ability to pay as you go for resources instead of having to size, forecast and purchase everything at once.

- Greatly reduces operating risks in that the complexities of managing infrastructure servers, storage and applications is handled by the Cloud provider allowing the business to focus on business activities instead of IT technical tasks.

- Provides transparency of cost for IT services directly aligned to usage and demand which is an area that many IT organizations have struggled with in the past. Businesses see great value in this (e.g. "now we can see what we are really paying for…").

- Provides economies of scale without requiring as much planning, forecasting and commitment to acquiring resources. Businesses just simply request more resource from the Cloud provider when they need it.

- Provides ubiquitous access to services. Services may be accessed from almost anywhere in the world without the need for installing hardware and software at local sites and then connecting them through a network.

- Provisioning of hardware and software resources is very quick. A new server, for example, could be requested and obtained in minutes versus the average 2-3 month delay most IT organizations encounter to acquire, purchase, install and configure their own services.

Cloud providers are able to make all this happen because a combination of newer technologies is being employed at a massive scale such that they can handle many customers at once. If you look inside a large Cloud provider, you will find heavy use of virtualization and automated processes. Delivery is handled in cookie cutter fashion such that services are delivered in the same way each time over and over for each customer.

Operating with IT Service Management disciplines is more critical than ever due to Cloud Computing. With this capability, the IT role is really shifting towards integration of services from many vendors providing their wares over the Cloud. Rather than engineer and build everything, IT focus is more on integrating all the parts and pieces to produce a holistic service that can be easily consumed by the business. All ITSM disciplines apply to make sure a service is being delivered without the need for the business to understand all the infrastructure services that underpin what they are getting.

At first, it may seem that Cloud Computing is just a rehash of the old Time-Sharing Services which have been available in the IT marketplace since the 1970's. With Time-Sharing you got mostly hardware provisioning. What is different now is the plethora of services combined with the pay-as-you-go on demand model that can deliver not only hardware, but an entire application stack and service if you so desire. A wide variety of applications, platforms or resources such as storage or processing can be had at attractive costs.

The diagram below shows a simple example of what is possible:

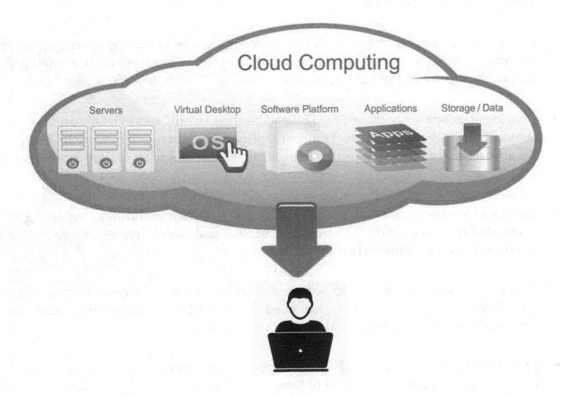

Cloud Service Offerings

When developing a service, the Service Strategy phase in the DevOps approach (see DevOps chapter) includes a key task to identify how the service will be sourced. What parts of the service should go into the Cloud? What items still need to stay within the business' IT infrastructure? If Cloud is used, how will those services be obtained? What support services will be used? To help with this, Cloud providers have segmented their service offerings typically in these ways:

- **Infrastructure As A Service (IaaS)**

  This covers the most basic kind of cloud services. Providers offer computing infrastructure and access to resources as a service to subscribers. These come in the form of virtualized servers, desktops, storage and networks. Subscribers pay as you go with these resources. They are provisioned quickly and remove the risks, time and costs associated with procuring, installing and operating these kinds of configuration items. Details of infrastructure like physical facilities, location, capacity scaling, backup, availability and security are handled by the provider.

- **Platform As A Service (PaaS)**

  This kind of service targets the application developer. Configuration items such as databases, GIS (Mapping) software, transaction middleware, and development environments are used by development staff to construct solutions. The provider maintains these platforms and makes access to them available via API, request or database call to developers. The provider may also include configuration items such as systems software, operating system, programming-language execution environments, databases, and web servers. Benefits include avoidance of the cost and complexity of buying and managing the underlying hardware and software layers. Developers still maintain control over their applications and configuration settings for the platforms they are subscribing to.

- **Software As A Service (SaaS)**

  This service targets the end customer. With this service, subscribers gain access to application software. Cloud providers manage the infrastructure and platforms that run the entire stack from hardware up through applications. The provider installs and operates application software in the cloud and subscribers access the software from their client devices. Subscribers do not manage the cloud infrastructure and platform where the application runs. This eliminates the need to install and run the application which simplifies maintenance and support.

Given the wide variety of Cloud-based offerings, development of services truly is a focus on integration. As a service is architected, a serious look needs to be taken to see if components in the architecture truly need to be developed by internal staff or leverage solutions that may already exist in the Cloud.

Cloud Deployment Models

As previously stated, the Cloud is essentially a service delivery mechanism. Within this, several popular moidels for delivery of Cloud services exist as shown below:

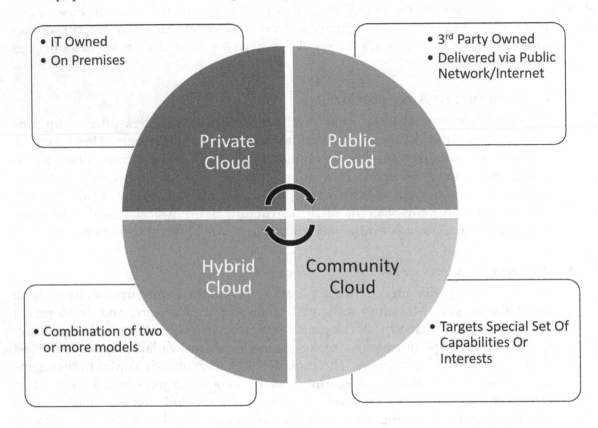

Private Cloud

With this model, the IT organization maintains their own Cloud infrastructure and offers Cloud services to the business units that they support. A variant of this would be to have that infrastructure managed by a third party supplier on behalf of IT, but essentially the IT organization is solely responsible for their Cloud infrastructure and services. With this, the IT organization builds their own Cloud infrastructure, virtualizes Cloud resources and delivers Cloud services through processes and automated technologies that IT owns and configures.

Pros:
- IT can fully own and control all aspects of their Cloud solution
- Avoids management concerns over security of data and applications
- May leverage resources and services that IT already has in place

Cons:
- Limited economies of scale
- Capital intensive including the need for physical footprint space
- No leverage of operating risk – IT is fully responsible

Public Cloud

With this model, Cloud services are provided by a third party supplier that owns and manages the Cloud infrastructure. Services are delivered over a public network (usually the internet) to many customers. Some providers may offer private secure network access to allay security concerns. The provider is not tied to any one particular customer or business entity. IT accesses Cloud services via a secure network connection. There is little or no need to provide any infrastructure.

Pros:
- Avoids investment in Cloud infrastructure
- Pay for what you use versus having to invest in an entire infrastructure
- Scaling and demand are handled by the supplier
- Much lower operating risk

Cons:
- Security concerns might exist with data and applications not on premises
- Performance issues might exist for sites in low bandwidth parts of the world
- Provider may make infrastructure changes on a schedule different than that preferred by the IT organization

Hybrid Cloud

This model is a combination of Private and Public models. With this model, the Private Cloud infrastructure on premises is bound with a Public Cloud. Each side is owned and operated distinctly. In some cases, delivery can be from any combination of two or more Cloud providers such that both are off premises but bound together. In either case, it lets IT integrate and extend their services across all Clouds in the Hybrid delivery model.

Pros:
- More flexibility where one of the other models won't do – for example, house sensitive data in the Private Cloud but connect to an application service running in the Public Cloud
- Provides a temporary capacity solution wherein the Private Cloud has temporary needs for more resources and uses a Public Cloud to provision them until no longer needed
- Flexibility for Cloud "bursting" when an application experiences unpredictable spikes in demand to handle sudden business demands like a major sale or special event

Cons:
- Requires more coordination with one or multiple Cloud providers
- Providers may make infrastructure changes at different times and on schedules different than that preferred by the IT organization

Community Cloud

With this model, IT and or multiple Cloud providers share infrastructure to target a specific set of capabilities or support services (e.g. collaboration across universities and schools, medical research).

Pros:
- Addresses special interest needs

Cons:
- Governance and agreement on standards and services could be an issue
- More costly than Public or Hybrid Cloud models

Cloud Security and Privacy

Security has always been a first and foremost issue with use of Public, Hybrid and Community Clouds for some time. Concerns exist like the following:

- The business may be bound by industry or regulatory constraints that prohibit where data is stored and accessed
- The service provider could access data residing their Cloud service at any time
- The service provider themselves might get hacked by an outside party
- Legal ownership of data may be in question – the provider may profit from that data
- The provider could accidentally or deliberately alter or even delete data
- The provider might share private information with third parties to meet legal requirements

To be fair, suppliers have made great strides in addressing security concerns over recent years. Options IT has can include:

- Taking advantage of supplier guarantees by which the supplier will fully indemnify the safety and warranty of their Cloud offerings
- Taking advantage of data encryption technologies such that data cannot be used by others
- Going to a hybrid delivery model to keep sensitive data on premises

Chapter
9

Leaning Out Service Transition

Operating In A World Of Rapid Change

Perhaps the most wasteful and slow set of management processes in all of IT exist with the Service Transition processes. These include:

- **Change Management** – processing requests for change, assessing, approving and scheduling changes to go live.

- **Release and Deployment Management** – undertaking activities to group changes into releases, configure, package and install releases into test, quality assurance and production environments.

- **Service Validation and Testing** – undertaking test activities on services and solutions to determine if defects exist.

- **Transition Planning and Support** – undertake activities to develop overall strategies and plan how solutions and changes will be migrated to the production environment.

- **Service Asset and Configuration Management** – undertaking activities to record, relate, maintain and communicate information about assets, infrastructure components, applications and other elements used to support and deliver services.

- **Knowledge Management** – undertaking activities to create, maintain and communicate knowledge across the IT infrastructure.

- **Change Evaluation** – undertaking activities to assess and predict the impact of changes on the business and compare actual business and technical outcomes attained to what was predicted.

High velocity ITSM is about employing agile and lean mechanisms to deliver faster and eliminate waste. Yet for Service Transition, consider these outcomes that are very typical of most IT organizations:

- Only 8% of IT organizations feel they have a "good" change management process
- Most IT organizations strongly feel that over 50% of changes that take place bypass change management controls
- Average turnaround to get approvals for changes is running anywhere from 9 to 22 business days
- Review and assessment of changes is resource intensive with Change Advisory Board meetings, frequent follow-up, filling out request forms and gathering information on what is about to be released
- Many releases incur long periods of time for testing – usually repeating the same testing activities over and over each time
- Over 80% of IT organizations report that the periods where there are the most incidents, service outages and support issues occur just after a new release has gone live
- Transition management processes in general are so inefficient that most agile and lean methods don't even discuss them, or worse yet, tout that you can bypass them by adopting those methods

So there is a major challenge with Service Transition management. Development staff are looking for ways to move fast, become agile, and get code and solutions into production without delays. Operations staff have opposite concerns about safety, stability and operating risk that might be lost by adopting to those methods.

So what is the right answer here? Hopefully this chapter sheds some light on where waste happens in Service Transition and what you might do about it. Addressing waste in Service Transition processes are a good first way of moving towards high velocity ITSM. It is in these processes where the most waste and delays occur in IT.

Lean Change Management

Of all the ITSM Management processes, Change Management is the most process intensive. Here is a good place to start down the path towards high velocity ITSM. A most common mistake made by many IT organizations is to develop lots of change processes and controls and then apply these to almost everything changing in the IT infrastructure. The process exists and must be used because it is needed to maintain control. Everyone must follow the process. The process is the same for everyone.

Lost in all this is that Change Management is really there for risk mitigation. If all changes could be implemented and communicated without defects and issues, then there would be no need to have a process in the first place. Not all changes have the same level of risk. Many are small, low impact changes that carry low levels of risk. Others are large, wide ranging and carry high levels of risk. IT continually implements this process with risk measures that are out of balance with the levels of risk to be protected against. This introduces unnecessary delays for many changes.

It may be a safe assumption that over 80% of all changes are small in nature, standard operating procedures, done every day carrying little risk. Maybe another 15% are of moderate risk. The last 5% or less are the really big ones that deserve lots of diligence and risk review. Yet IT, employs means and methods used to deal with higher risk changes across the board to almost all changes. This is where the imbalance lies. As will be seen in this chapter, the suggestion is start the Change Management process with a focus on risk, then employ the right level of control processes based on the risk level that exists.

The Eight Deadly Wastes chart below (See ITSM Lean Toolkit Chapter) has been filled out for Change Management and summarizes common places where waste exists. It also provides some ideas on how you might address the waste identified.

	Category	Areas Of Waste	What Might Be Done
	Inventory	• Change records are left in the Change Management system long after they were completed or abandoned.	• Automate removal of RFCs for which there has been no action taken for a specified period (e.g. 30 days) • Auto close changes within 3-5 business days once they have been implemented

	Category	Areas Of Waste	What Might Be Done
	Talent	• Heavy consumption of skilled resources for CAB meetings and technical reviews. • Those assessing and improving the change are highly dependent on skills of those implementing the change – executives may be in approval loop but are helpless to make informed decision unless team below them has agreed (This is why Emergency changes are so dangerous). • Support staff are not always aware of the changes that have been made by others. • Some change representatives sit in a CAB meeting for long periods of time listening to changes for others before they get to discuss theirs.	• Push as much review work outside the CAB meeting as possible through electronic reviews and approvals • Don't waste CAB meeting time discussing change that have unanimously been approved or rejected • Limit reviews to only those changes that score in the higher risk categories • Ensure review activities are included as agile work items that make up a Sprint or Release • Schedule CAB meetings such that high risk changes are discussed early and at a set time to maximize people's time and participation. • Inventory and publicize a listing of all changes that will be taking place and categorize these by service being delivered versus technology – e.g. can see all the changes taking place for Email Support or Sales Support (or all services if that applies).

	Category	Areas Of Waste	What Might Be Done
	Waiting	• Majority of lead time is spent waiting for approvals. • Changes have to be scheduled so delays are incurred waiting for open time slots to implement.	• Aggressively drive and implement Standard Changes as these require no approval time • Limit who needs to approve based on risk as described above • Change Advisory Board (CAB) should vote outside of the CAB meeting • CAB meetings should focus time on changes where there is disagreement versus every change submitted • Only address higher risk changes in CAB meetings – low risk changes should be approved by the Change Management team within hours not days. • Align request for change with each agile development iteration such that any needed requirements are included as agile work items. • Auto create requests for change from development tools to pre-populate change descriptions, configuration information, test results and other items. • Use of Continuous Release, Testing and Deployment mechanisms can serve to reduce delays for scheduling and moving things into production (see chapter on Agile).

	Category	Areas Of Waste	What Might Be Done
	Motion	• Many IT organizations vary their adherence to the process by technology team – in many cases people bypass the process altogether. • The process is handled differently by each support team.	• Automate interfaces between the Change Management system and development tools such that it is hard for people to handle changes differently. • Pre-score changes by risk first as described earlier and force a diligence path as described before.

	Category	Areas Of Waste	What Might Be Done
⊘	Defects	• Support and development staff bypass the change management process • Changes may sometimes fail leading to incidents, outages and other events that create unplanned costs and delays • Some RFCs are submitted late or at the last minute with urgent needs robbing IT of ability to conduct due diligence. • 70% of incidents are related to changes. Rework to fix these, re-do a bad change is at high levels. • Requestors many times provide scant information about what is really changing – they communicate in highly technical terms that few others outside their team understand. • Most IT organizations do not report on change defect rates. • Impact of changes is poorly done and IT rarely communicates or understands the true business impact of a change.	• Report service incidents and defects by service owner and make results public across IT – since most incidents are caused by changes, this will get noticed and put pressure on individuals to conform • Automate generation of change requests from development tools as this will make it impossible for developers to work without making changes visible • Defects typically occur when human hands are involved – automate implementation of changes and releases to the greatest extent possible. • Categorize and classify changes by service as this aligns each change with the business service it impacts. • Make sure that failed changes are reported as defects. This includes changes that failed after they went live, changes that failed to deploy and changes that had to be rescheduled. Publish defect rates by each service and service owner.

	Category	Areas Of Waste	What Might Be Done
	Transportation	• Requestors have to document lots of information about a change. • Requestors have to re-key information about their change into an RFC form (e.g. what CIs are impacted). • Improperly filled out RFCs get rejected and sent back to requestor for rework. • Information from RFCs and assessments of them is typically recreated in different formats for CAB meetings or executive reviews.	• Limit what requestors have to provide based on the risk level their change falls into. • Take a hard look at change request forms to remove items that no one cares about. • Automate population of common fields from other information sources that already exist such as Active Directory for requestor contact information. • Avoid complicated and restrictive forms or screens that make it hard to enter information (e.g. input field has no word wrap). • Don't force users to have to rekey information from another system into the change management system. • Automate generation of change requests from development tools that pre-populate change request forms with change information, configuration information, design drawings and other items as much as possible. • Automate production of reports and information used for CAB meetings from change data in the change management system.

	Category	Areas Of Waste	What Might Be Done
	Overprocessing	• Lack of focus on standard changes – many changes incur unnecessary reviews, or require lots of informational input even though their risk is low. • Risk assessments are done far too late in the process. Risk is only assessed as a check item on the RFC form after a complete RFC is filled out. • Too many change types that make the change process more complicated and harder to use.	• Focus heavily on production of Standard Changes to reduce process overhead. • Do change risk assessment first and then send the RFC down the workflow path that best deals with that level of risk. Use the right amount of process for the right amount of risk. • Utilize the small list of change categories presented earlier in this chapter.
	Overproduction	• Many IT organizations produce large numbers of RFCs that in turn create a backlog of delays waiting to get into the Change Management system. • Far too many changes are incurring lots of process and approval overhead even though they are low in risk.	• Bundle changes together into a release and create an RFC only for the release being implemented. This can greatly cut down the number of RFCs that need to be processed. • Batch RFCs by risk level – this way multiple RFCs can be handled much faster and together as a group versus one by one. • Prioritize RFCs such that the most urgent ones get ahead of the line.

Given all the efficiency issues around Change Management, a suggested approach is presented in some detail as to how it may be more effectively operated:

1) Start the first part of the RFC form with questions about which risks exist with the change (see example to follow). These should be pre-marked to YES to indicate that

the highest level of risk exists. Requestors must physically set the answers to NO (prevents laziness to just quickly submit the form).

2) A scoring mechanism assesses the answers provided and places the change into a Minor, Normal or Major change risk category.

3) Minor risk changes fly through the process very quickly, Normal and Major categories will incur more diligence.

4) Note that changes that will be implemented through automated mechanisms will much lower in risk than those implemented with human intervention – therefore the more automated implementation activities are, the better.

5) Those scored as a Minor Change have an option to mark the change as a Standard Change for future use. Review activities to approve changes as Standard happen outside the change request workflow.

6) The number of RFC fields to be filled in, and the amount of information to be provided by the requestor should vary based on risk score. Those who score Minor only need to fill out basic information. Higher risks require more documentation and proof of artifacts such as test results.

7) Change approval activities are aligned based on the risk score. A Minor Change may need only a Change Manager approval. Other levels require the CAB to approve and maybe even key executives.

Here are some examples of how this might get set up in the Change Management system:

Below presents an example of the risk questions and scoring. These would be presented first, before the requestor provides any more information about their change.

Risk	Yes	No	Yes Value
Could violate an SLA agreement or cause a degradation of service	X		2
Requires a client facing outage to implement	X		5
Could trigger a security risk	X		7
Impacts a component other systems and services are dependent on	X		5
Cannot be backed out	X		7
Requires coordination across multiple teams to implement	X		5
First time a change of this kind has been implemented	X		3

Risk	Yes	No	Yes Value
Has been implemented in the past but with failures	X		5
Impacts a key customer or multiple customers	X		5
Can't be implemented within maintenance window	X		7
Can't be tested prior to implementation	X		10
Requires customer validation to complete	X		5
TOTAL:			66

In the above, the Yes Values can be whatever you want to set them to. The sum of the values determines the risk classification. Calculation of the scores is done behind the scenes. The requestor only sees the question, YES and NO. They get instant feedback as to the risk rating.

Based on the risk rating, a Change Category is identified. The table below presents one example:

Score Range	Risk Category	Approvals Required
0-5	Minor Change and requestor can submit as a candidate for standard change for future use	• Change Manager • CAB approval (done outside the approval workflow for this change) if requestor wants to make this a Standard Change
6-10	Minor Change	• Change Manager
11-20	Normal Change	• Change Manager • Change Advisory Board
21 or Higher	Major Change	• Change Manager • Change Advisory Board • Executive Management

Once the above is in place, you can then set the appropriate process workflows and evidence required for each Change Category. For approvals, only proof and a link to information is required. As an example, a Major Change may require proof of successful testing. In this case, Change Management should only be looking for a signoff from the testing team.

Try to avoid having requestors re-document information about their change whenever possible. ALM information should auto-flow things like configuration item information, test results and design documentation. In a high velocity ITSM world, these activities should auto-flow documentation and results to Change Management without requestors having to do extra administrative work.

Try to avoid having lots of change categories. This just makes the process unnecessarily complex. The categories suggested below keep things simple.

Change Category	Description	Velocity Of Approval	Approvals Required
Standard	Done frequently, low risk, low impact, standard operating procedures that never causes an incident. These should be invoked by drop-down list in the Change Management system. They are entered initially by requesting a change that is low risk and requesting it to be a standard change. Approval to go on the list comes from the CAB.	Immediate	• No approval needed
Minor	Scores as a low risk change. Requires only minimal information.	4-8 hours	• Change Manager only

Change Category	Description	Velocity Of Approval	Approvals Required
Normal	Scores as a moderate risk change. Requires a CAB review and a moderate amount of documentation.	Up to 2 business days if all CAB members electronically agree else up to 9 business days if they don't. Note that the latter could be faster if the CAB holds more than one meeting throughout the week.	• Change Manager • Change Advisory Board (CAB)
Major	Scores as a high risk change. Requires a CAB and Executive Review plus evidence of successful tests and avoidance of operating risk.	9 Business days or more. You want to really slow these down to avoid major issues. Submission of change requests at the soonest possible time can help reduce delays.	• Change Manager • Change Advisory Board • Executive Management
Latent	This category is reserved for changes discovered after the fact. They can be submitted by anyone when there is discovery that a change has taken place without a corresponding RFC. Information required is simple and basic. The changes should still be scored for risk. No approvals are required.	Immediate, but the change management team should review and report these on a periodic basis to brief executives and understand why they occurred.	• None required

Change Category	Description	Velocity Of Approval	Approvals Required
Emergency	ANY change that has to go in before normal change management processes can be applied to assess and approve it.	As soon as possible. Emergency changes for which there is not enough time to get the executive approval should be implemented right away and the change categorized as Latent at a later time.	• Requires approval of at least 1 executive.

Some IT organizations implement categories like "Urgent". Try to avoid these. They serve no other purpose than to hide IT issues from management. They rob IT from being able to do proper due diligence, create additional risk and act as a means to go around the process. They also greatly confuse IT support staff as to when they should be applied. Set a policy that ANY change that needs to be processed outside the normal policy and timeframes should be handled as an Emergency Change no matter what the reason for the late submittal.

Lean Release and Deployment Management

Release and Deployment Management is perhaps the second biggest area where IT waste is found. Typical issues in most IT organizations include:

- Deployment of IT solutions to production with ill preparation to operate them at acceptable cost and risk
- Lack of automation with deployment tasks leading to errors and outages
- Delays related to testing and quality assurance activities
- Deploying solutions in a "big bang" fashion that introduces higher levels of operating risk

The Eight Deadly Wastes chart below (See ITSM Lean Toolkit Chapter) has been filled out for Release and Deployment Management and summarizes common places where waste exists. It also provides some ideas on how you might address the waste identified.

	Category	Areas Of Waste	What Might Be Done
	Inventory	• Producing new releases of software that are not really needed	• If these exist, identify them and retire them
	Talent	• Utilizing skilled resources to work on repetitive simple deployment tasks that could be done better automated or with less skilled staff	• Automate deployment activities to eliminate the need for manual hands-on work to the greatest extent possible • Consider out-tasking deployment activities to a third party that can handle activities efficiently and at lower cost
	Waiting	• Extensive delays from the time a release is first introduced until it is deployed to all those who will use it • Delays introduced by releases that are dependent on other releases which have not been completed or scheduled to deploy	• Utilize the DevOps approach described earlier in this book to have operations staff work with development at the earliest stages so that release activities can be completed at the same point that solution are ready to go live • Utilize the Agile approaches described earlier in this book such that releases and all their dependent releases are deployed together as a single unit

	Category	Areas Of Waste	What Might Be Done
	Motion	• Use of manual deployment activities such as installing media into desktops • Releases that require staff to be physically present at local sites to do manual installs and configuration work	• Utilize configuration and software distribution tools to automate and "push" software and configurations out to local sites without the need for physical presence • Consider use of 3rd parties for hands-on work at local sites if needed
	Defects	• Releases that go live with application bugs. • Releases that go live that can't be operated at acceptable cost and risk. • Releases that go live that cannot be effectively monitored for availability and proper operating state. • Releases that are not properly packaged and staged for deployment • Releases that go live for which users of the release are not properly trained.	• Utilize the DevOps approach described earlier in this book to have operations staff work with development at the earliest stages so that release activities can be completed at the same point that solution are ready to go live • Test release activities before they are scheduled to go live • Use pilot releases to blunt the impact of failures and shake out release issues before general deployment begins

	Category	Areas Of Waste	What Might Be Done
	Transportation	• Releases that are improperly staged such that delays occur from network bandwidth or processing issues • Releases that are constantly moved from Development to Test to QA (Quality Assurance) to Production.	• Utilize the Automation concepts described earlier in this book to handle code movement with Continuous Release, Testing and Deployment facilities • Utilize software staging servers located at local sites to more effectively handle bandwidth constraints (deploy once across the network to stage locally then many times from local site server to deployment targets
	Overprocessing	• Undertaking extensive quality assurance activities and reviews for low impact/low risk releases.	• If release and deployment activities are low risk and have low impact, then don't force them through long lengthy review and QA processes
	Overproduction	• Issuing too many releases.	• Bundle changes together into a release and create an RFC only for the release being implemented. • Bundle releases together to reduce their overall number

Shifting Left With Orchestrated Deployments

Agile and DevOps approaches can be leveraged to put lots of velocity into Release and Deployment activities. The key focus is on production of solutions that are always in a releasable state made possible through continuous release, continuous testing and continuous deployment mechanisms. The goal is to automate deployments such that they reduce or eliminate the need for human intervention to the greatest extent possible. The focus is on production of code that is always in a releasable state with automatic deployment through continuous release, continuous testing and continuous deployment.

A model for accomplishing this is shown below:

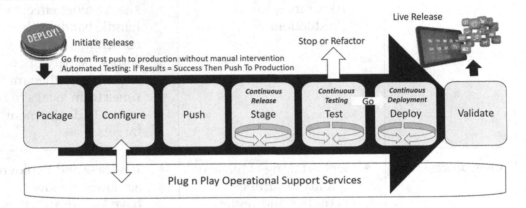

When it is agreed that a release is to be produced, the development team initiates an automated deployment request for the code they have produced. Fulfillment is automated. The code is packaged, configured and pushed to a Release staging area. The staging area is always available and stocked with production ready code to be deployed and maintains releases in their entirety.

On a periodic basis, releases are then deployed into a Continuous Test environment. This environment is always up and running. It continually cycles through automated testing scripts looking for signs of defects. If a defect is uncovered, then the automated testing scripts throw back the code to the development team for repair. If no defect are found, and all scripts run successfully, then the release is pushed out to the Deployment environment. From here, Releases get automatically distributed and deployed out to the production environment. Again, this is accomplished through deployment scripts. Deployments could be immediate, or held back and released at set intervals that are scheduled.

When deployments are executed, end users always get the latest release from the Deployment environment. In a high velocity world, users are always on the latest release at the time they receive a deployment. There is no deployment of older releases or holding groups of users back from the latest release. That only complicates support, creates delays, introduces costly upgrade efforts and costs more to maintain.

The Plug and Play Operational Support services are integrated with each release. These represent common IT service support functions like handling incidents, requests, monitoring and other support needs. These are bundled into services and provided to the development team for managing the solution on an ongoing basis as described in the chapter on DevOps.

Continuous Release, Testing and Deployment

A key objective of ALM, Agile and Lean IT is to embrace rapid change and eliminate waste in delivery of IT services. One of the biggest challenges in doing this is in the Service Transition stage. Processes like Change Management, Release Management, Deployment, Validation and Testing are necessary to effectively deploy service changes and protect live services while these activities are happening. The time and effort to execute these needed tasks traditionally introduces many delays. So how to best deal with rapid change? Can these processes still operate, but in a much more efficient fashion?

The answer is yes, but with a much different way of operating. Rather than trigger these processes serially each time a change or release is introduced, release, testing and deployment will operate in a continuous and automated fashion. Rather than operate in serial fashion they will operate in parallel. The industry has been adopting this new approach as Continuous Release, Continuous Testing and Continuous Deployment.

The diagram below illustrates how these work to deploy solutions into production:

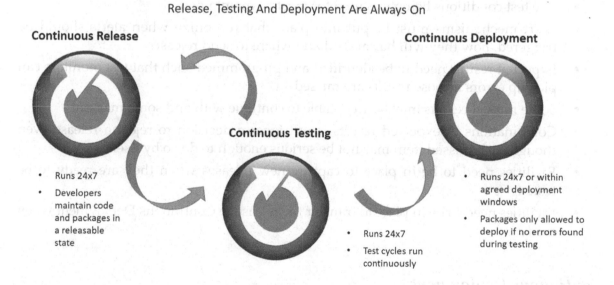

Release, Testing And Deployment Are Always On

Continuous Release

- Runs 24x7
- Developers maintain code and packages in a releasable state

Continuous Testing

- Runs 24x7
- Test cycles run continuously

Continuous Deployment

- Runs 24x7 or within agreed deployment windows
- Packages only allowed to deploy if no errors found during testing

Continuous Release

The release environment is always on and always has the latest release of the solution. For applications, source code is kept in a source code repository as it is being worked on. When ready, that code is then propagated to the release environment. Code may be propagated at any time. The release environment always has the most current set of releasable code. Branching (described later in this chapter) allows developers to work on multiple parts of a release independently and in parallel and then merge their work back to the main release when ready.

Continuous Testing

This upends the traditional testing approach that it has used for a long time. With Continuous Testing, a test facility is in operation all the time. The facility executes test runs and monitors results in a highly automated fashion. New releases can be thrown at this facility at any point in time. As a release enters the facility it is automatically thrown into a series of automated test cycles. The facility monitors for defects and bugs. If they are found, an alert is fired off and the release goes back to the development team. It proceeds no further.

If the release gets through the entire test run successfully, then it proceeds on to the Continuous Deployment function.

The effort to maintain a continuous test operation should not be underestimated. What you gain in speed requires close and constant attention. Here are some aspects that need to be considered:

- Automated test scripts need to be developed and maintained all the time
- As changes are introduced with each new release, automated test scripts must be updated to recognize additional items that need to be tested for
- Test data must be tightly controlled and maintained
- The test conditions being executed for must be maintained
- Alert mechanisms must be put into place that recognize when alerts should be triggered, how they will be handled and where to send releases
- Expected results need to be identified and programmed such that test monitors can pick up errors if those results are missed
- Some missed results may be acceptable to continue with and some may not
- Combinations of expected results may trigger a decision to reject a release even though each missed item may not be serious enough to do so by itself
- Facilities need to be in place to capture new releases when they are ready to be tested
- Facilities need to be in place to transfer the release to Continuous Deployment when ready

Continuous Deployment

As releases successfully exit Continuous Testing, they are automatically staged for deployment. At this point, automated activities take place to configure, package and stage releases for deployment into production.

Don't confuse Continuous Release with Continuous Deployment! It is not a good practice to continuously deploy. There are many reasons where releases may need to be held back for a period of time. Some of these are:

- Users are not ready to absorb the changes or need training before a new release can go live

- Increased risks may occur if deploying during peak business periods (e.g. end of year closing, or holiday sales cycle)

- Network bandwidth constraints prohibit widespread deployment – this is a typical problem in some areas of the world where bandwidth capacity is poor

- The deployment may require approvals, extra validation or a compliance audit before it can take place

- Physical activities need to occur at sites that are targets for the deployment

- Business imposed change freeze may be in place in which no changes are allowed to occur.

Lean Asset and Configuration Management

The issues with Asset and Configuration Management are not so much having a clunky wasteful process as it is an ineffective process. IT complaints in this area usually center on lack of reliable asset or configuration information. This can lead to:

- Longer development times as IT staff has to find and research configurations over and over for deployments or build of new services
- Incidents and outages related to implementation of solutions that depended on one set of configuration information when really something else was in production
- Incidents and outages related to implementation of changes where the full impact of what was being changed was not accurately identified
- Fines and penalties for not accurately accounting for assets and configuration items that have been used but not licensed for

Recognizing these issues, IT will tend to put controls and processes in place that may be overly burdensome on the IT support organization. Examples taken from real IT organizations include:

- Implementation of a configuration management system that forced everyone making an infrastructure change to manually record every configuration item into the configuration management system with little control or standards. The end result: millions of configuration item records in the database, unreliable information that no one used, slower and labor intensive change process and high frustration across all IT staff.
- Unreliable asset information that forced an IT organization to undertake labor heavy physical inventory counts every 6 months
- An IT organization that tracked asset and configuration information at such unnecessary levels of detail that they were buried in useless information that no one looked at

The Eight Deadly Wastes chart below (See ITSM Lean Toolkit Chapter) has been filled out for Asset and Configuration Management and summarizes common places where waste exists. It also provides some ideas on how you might address the waste identified.

	Category	Areas Of Waste	What Might Be Done
	Inventory	• Over scoping Asset and Configuration Management such that many CIs are being tracked that no one cares about • Using CI types when attributes may be more efficient (e.g. separate CIs for PC, Mouse, Keyboard and Cables when one CI type will do where Keyboard, Mouse and Cables are attributes of that type)	• Remove types that no one cares about • Collapse CI information into fewer types by using attributes
	Talent	• Knowledge of configurations is highly dependent on specific people	• Utilize a configuration management system and work with key technology stakeholders to populate it • Utilize asset and configuration tools that "discover" the infrastructure and report back – this removes the dependency on people
	Waiting	• Delays related to manually updating CI and asset information before releases can go live	• Utilize Application Lifecycle Management (ALM) tools to automate the movement of asset and configuration information directly from development into configuration repositories • Utilize discovery tools to auto-populate asset and configuration management repositories and information

	Category	Areas Of Waste	What Might Be Done
	Motion	• Physically taking CI information from one system and entering it in another configuration system	• Utilize Application Lifecycle Management (ALM) tools to automate the movement of configuration information directly from development into configuration repositories
	Defects	• CI information that is incorrect • CI information that does not match production	• Conduct periodic asset and CI audits to validate information accuracy against that observed in the live environment • Utilize asset and configuration discovery tools that can report back on configuration changes against the original configuration baseline
	Transportation	• Delays related to researching configurations because the information is not available	• Utilize a configuration management system with flexible reporting such that research activities can be done quickly and easily
	Overprocessing	• Providing asset and configuration reports that no one looks at or are not needed • Collecting information on assets and configuration items that no one really uses	• Eliminate reports, CI Types and related information that no one looks at or uses

	Category	Areas Of Waste	What Might Be Done
	Overproduction	• Centralizing asset and configuration information when a federated approach might be more efficient	• Consider using a federated approach that recognizes disparate asset and configuration repositories and links that information back to a central source

When it comes to optimizing how asset and configuration management information is maintained, consider the following general guidelines:

- Manual audits can serve as validation efforts to periodically check information accuracy but should not be depended on for populating asset and configuration repositories
- A heavy focus should be on automating the creation and movement of asset configuration information flow – this means using reliable automated discovery functions and electronically moving information to systems that need it
- Assets and configuration item information created by development staff in the course of building or maintaining a service should electronically flow into asset and configuration management systems without the need for manual re-entry of information
- Use of configuration information can be active with Declarative Configuration Management technologies versus just passive – see next section of this chapter.

Declarative Configuration Management

The next generation of Configuration Management is now evolving. Historically, configuration management activities strove to provide information about configuration items and their status. With Declarative Configuration Management, configuration information is stored in a declarative state that can then be compiled and executed. When compiled, it translates configuration management information into scripts that then automate the building and provisioning of the configurations described. In short, it transforms configuration management from merely providing information on configurations to actually building and installing them. There is no need to specify OS commands or undertake manual provisioning activities.

The diagram below demonstrates use of this technology:

```
Configuration WebSiteConfig
{
    param ( $NodeName ) |

    Node $NodeName
    {
        WindowsFeature IIS
        {
            Ensure = "Present"
            Name = "Web-Server"
        }

        WindowsFeature ASP
        {
            Ensure = "Present"
            Name = "Web-Asp-Net45"
        }
    }
}
```

Configuration information, as shown above, is documented as "code" which specifies the configuration items to be installed and how they will be configured. This "code" is then executed which kicks off and automates installation and configuration actions. This approach provides tremendous gains in speed and accuracy as little or no human intervention is needed. It ensures that configurations are implemented the same way every time.

Containerization

There are often many challenges that stand in the way of easily moving applications through the development cycle and eventually into production. Besides the actual work of developing applications to respond appropriately in each environment, there are issues with tracking down dependencies, scaling the application, and updating individual components without affecting the entire application.

Containerization technologies can serve to more effectively address many of these problems. With Containerization, applications are broken up into smaller functional components. Each component is then, packaged individually with all its dependencies, and deployed as a single unit. Scaling and updating applications to meet different demands is also simplified. Just deploy more containers.

Containers work by wrapping and bundling applications into a complete filesystem that contains everything needed to run such as code, runtime libraries, system tools, and system libraries. This is then abstracted from the underlying OS and hardware via a Containerization Engine. The engine abstracts all the operating system and hardware details from the Container. Containers can be deployed to almost any platform without having to change application code.

The concept of Containers is similar to use of Virtualized Machines. With Virtual Machines you are provisioning an entire virtual server and guest operating system upon which applications will run. With a Container, you are only provisioning the application without need for an entire virtual machine. From the Virtualization chapter in this book, remember that Virtual Machines are managed in their entirety: application, binaries and libraries, and an entire guest operating system. With Containerization, only the Container itself needs to be managed which is much less on systems overhead.

The diagram below shows the difference between Containers versus Virtualized Machine solutions:

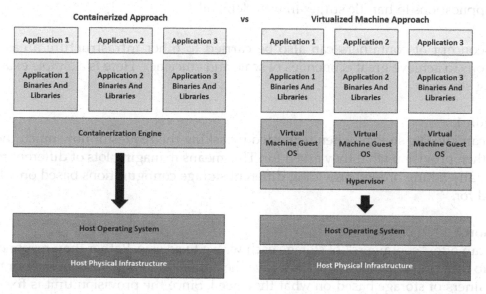

Containers are standardized. They connect to a host and to anything outside of the container through a Containerization Engine using defined interfaces. The Containerization Engine abstracts the details of the host operating system and hardware from the Container. What does this all mean? Applications are completely separated from operating systems and hardware. Deploy a containerized application once and you can deploy it anywhere over and over no matter what platform is the target. With Containerization, applications are not reliant upon details about the underlying host's resources or architecture. To the host, every container is a black box. It does not care about the details of the application inside.

By separating and abstracting the interfaces between the host system and the container, scaling is much easier. A set of containers used by a small number of users may be placed onto a small server. As the number of users goes up, additional containers can be deployed onto multiple servers are a large server array.

Maintenance, patching and versioning of applications is simpler. These activities would be contained within the container itself. Configurations of containers use Declarative Configuration management functions (see previous chapter) to configure and deploy containers. In this way, the same identical container image is always produced when deployed no matter what platform it is being deployed upon. Configurations may be baselined and versioned for easier management.

Impact on deployment activities carries a lot of benefits:

- Labor tasks to set up developer environments, provision new instances, and make copies of production code are minimalized or not needed – containers can be deployed to and run on any new endpoint running a Container Engine

- Deployments go much faster since you are replicating the same containers across all target environments
- More frequent software updates can be done because the deployment tasks are the same and less activities are required for each deployment
- Provisioning of Containers can be done very quickly making it easy to scale applications to handle surges in user demand

The concept of containers can also be carried to other infrastructure areas besides applications to achieve great economies of scale and efficiency. Here is a simple example for allocating storage:

Option 1
You can allocate storage when requested by asking the requestor how much they need and then provision what they asked for. This means managing lots of different requests. Manually taking orders, providing different storage configurations based on what they asked for.

Option 2
You can offer "containers" of storage each with a fixed size. Rather than respond one by one to differing requests, requestors have the option of taking one container or multiple containers of storage based on what they need. Since the provision unit is fixed, it can easily be automated without human intervention. Capacity management of storage is easier.

Take the above example even further. Think about containers that have whole operating systems, platforms, and databases that could be deployed as a single unit. The need to develop differing configurations goes away and deployment becomes more cookie cutter. Deploy the whole container and everything goes with it. When users need more, they just get more containers.

Challenges With Continuous Deployment

In a high velocity world, users are always on the latest release at the time they receive a deployment. There is no deployment of older releases or holding groups of users back from the latest release. That only complicates support, creates delays, introduces costly upgrade efforts and costs more to maintain.

One big change in the industry is to deploy software (many times via cloud) and always keep it on the latest version. Changes are introduced in much smaller increments, disruption is less, and the need to synchronize releases and versions becomes much less. To deal with this, changes in how IT manages more frequent and rapid changes is key.

Continuous Deployment has a lot of benefits. It smooths out the constant boom and bust of major upgrade projects. In theory, it allows the business to always be on the latest software and therefor quickly adapt to business changes. Software is always secure, up to date and under warranty. It promotes agile operations within IT towards change. Gone are technology roadmaps, upgrade cycles, managing upgrade dependencies and all those complexities that contribute to IT management headaches.

However, there are challenges with this:

- Users are constantly receiving changes

- Look and feel of services and applications is a moving target – new changes in appearance, menu items and functionality is there one day and somewhere else the next

- If services are being provisioned from external parties (such as a Cloud SaaS Provider), IT and the business have little or no control over the frequency and timing of new releases

- Some business restrictions may present further challenges such as need for regulatory approval of IT changes or a change freeze period to protect services at critical times or simply have testing and quality assurance activities that introduce delays

- An IT cultural shift needs to happen to transform from fixed point in time releases and upgrades to agile thinking, smaller increments of change and constantly upgrading infrastructure

Some strategies that are being employed by IT organizations to deal with all this are as follows:

- **Executive sponsorship is key.** Executives need to demonstrate support for Continuous Deployment models and the business challenges they represent. This can't just be an "IT thing" to manage.

- **Testing and quality assurance needs to be continuous as well.** Continuous testing and deployment facilities need to be in place as described earlier in this chapter.

- **Each impacted business unit will require an Early Adopter role.** Business units will have to employ a new role of Early Adopter who will receive and use new releases before they are deployed to the rest of the Business Unit.

- **Testing and Quality Assurance processes need to be optimized.** Traditional models of testing and quality assurance that run weeks or even months need to be aggressively changed so they don't become bottlenecks. Aggressively automating these activities to increase their velocity will be key.

- **Minimize hold-offs on solution changes.** Holding off on changes may be harder to do because suppliers will not support back releases of their solutions. They may provide a small grace window, but the days when old releases were supported for years after new ones were made available are fast disappearing. Holding off may result in a reversal back to the days of big-bang releases and running on unsupported software.

- **Executive sponsorship is key.** IT will be most successful if the company undergoes a company-wide organizational shift towards managing processes efficiently and fluidly. This IT shift requires not only a significant change in thinking, but also more upfront investment in operational refinement and process automations.

- **There is also a cultural shift that needs to happen.** There is a lot of apprehension around the thought of continuous updates and possible loss of control. Both IT and the business need to be carefully managed and communicate with to avoid rejection and other problems.

- **IT management processes will have to be redefined.** There are many processes (e.g., procurement, license management, asset management, service requests and service integration) that will need to be redesigned to support the much more frequent needs for managing your IT landscape on a continuous basis.

- **Configuration and Asset management must include a central place to store all the end user states (current state vs. available state).** From a technical perspective, this means you will need to ensure you are on top of your asset information at all times and be proactive rather than reactive!

Most software vendors utilize a continuous deployment model where release occur frequently and in small increments, usually on a monthly basis. Since many businesses are skittish about simply accepting changes as they come, vendors will issue their software with several options:

- **Option 1** – get the software and all planned changes to it for the given month
- **Option 2** – get the software without any planned changes
- **Option 3** – get the software, all planned changes and any experimental changes the developers are working on

By deploying with these options, businesses can hold back, just a bit, so they can get ready for the coming changes. Vendors may allow users to defer updates for as long as a year, but recognize that if you do this, all benefits of agile deployment go out the window. The amount of change has piled up similar to what you might experience with a yearly software upgrade.

The trick is to deploy changes as quickly as reasonable and mitigate the risks while doing so. This can be done by using the role of Early Adopter. This can be a volunteer role. Early Adopters expect that software they get may have a higher risk of bugs and issues.

Once Early Adopters are in place you can use a deployment model similar to the one pictured below:

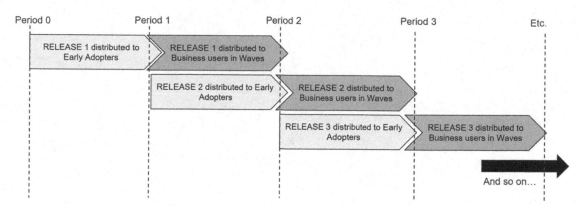

With this, establishing Early Adopters in each business unit is key. They will receive new software plus any planned updates. After a set period of time, the release used by the Early Adopters then goes out to the rest of the business unit. At that point, the Early Adopters then get the same release, but with planned changes for the next cycle. After that period ends, those changes then go out to the business and so on.

Leaning Out Service Operation

Leaning Out Incident Management

The Eight Deadly Wastes chart below (See ITSM Lean Toolkit Chapter) has been filled out for the Service Desk and handling of incident and request tickets. This summarizes common places where waste exists. It also provides some ideas on how you might address the waste identified.

	Category	Areas Of Waste	What Might Be Done
📦	Inventory	• Production of incident and request reports that no one reads or acts upon • Production of incident data and history that is not used to improve services	• Stop producing reports that no one needs or looks at • Reduce data fields or other report items that are not actually used • Align ticket classifications to services and ensure impacted configuration items are identified separately on each incident ticket

	Category	Areas Of Waste	What Might Be Done
	Talent	• Onboarding of new employees that consumes a lot Service Desk administrative time and resources to bring the employee in and up to speed • Manual processing of common requests that happen frequently over and over	• Aggressively utilize self-service and automation to eliminate need for calls to the Service Desk for frequently used requests • Institute a demand process to model and schedule call agent staff based on historical and forecasted ticket volumes • Monitor call agent effectiveness to ensure tickets are being handled promptly and efficiently such that they do not slow down the ticket pipeline
		• Too many or not enough call agents to handle demand • High levels of staff turnaround	• Aggressively work to push call agent onboarding and off boarding tasks to HR and training functions to minimize Service Desk administrative overhead • Aggressively work to keep staff morale at high levels and provide learning and promotion opportunities to minimize turnaround

	Category	Areas Of Waste	What Might Be Done
	Waiting	• Researching solutions or how-to information to assist users • Waiting for support teams to respond when calls are escalated • Long call queues and wait times • Long waits to get incidents resolved or requests fulfilled • Call agents that spend too much time trying to resolve tickets that should have been escalated much faster • Long incident resolution times • Long request fulfillment times • User delays for escalated tickets where they have to wait for technicians to call who end up asking similar questions or more detail about what took place	• Aggressively push service owners and Level2/3 support staff to provide knowledge and scripts to empower the Service Desk to resolve issues at first call • Publish first call rates for all service owners and staff teams and reward those with high first call rates • Publish incident and request resolution times for all service owners and staff teams and reward those with the least delays • Ensure call agents have easily understood criteria for when to escalate tickets • Consider use of chat or other alternative channels for support • Consider use of 3rd parties who may be more effective and timely • See if service solutions can be better designed for user friendliness such as adding "Helpful Hints" to screens and fields they work with • Consider use of Walk-In Clinics located in user areas where they can just walk in and get help and support

	Category	Areas Of Waste	What Might Be Done
⇅	Motion	• Many touches and hand-off points to process an incident • High number of incidents that do not get resolved at first call	• Aggressively push service owners and Level2/3 support staff to provide knowledge and scripts to empower the Service Desk to resolve issues at first call • Aggressively institute self-service knowledge and support to avoid service desk calls for help
⊘	Defects	• Incident and request tickets closed even though the incident is not resolved or the request not fulfilled • Dropped calls • High call abandon rates • Tickets wrongly classified • Wrong incident resolution categories used • Incident descriptions and resolution solutions not adequately documented and recorded • Lost incident or request tickets • Tickets escalated to the wrong support teams	• Ensure ticket closure processes audit tickets for proper classifications and closure categories before they are closed • Validate resolution of incidents or fulfillment of requests before tickets are closed • Conduct regular spot checks of incident and request tickets for proper documentation and classification and follow up with individuals when errors are found • Aggressively fix and resolve call management system errors and defects • Validate that staffing levels are in line with ticket demand volumes • Align ticket classifications with support teams to automate who gets escalated to versus depending on call agent expertise

	Category	Areas Of Waste	What Might Be Done
	Transportation	• Delays caused by tickets that get bounced from one support team to another with little ownership for resolution or fulfillment • Users having to fill out long ticket forms with information that is seldom used • Users having to repeat their issue over and over as calls get escalated	• Ensure that the Service Desk owns tickets completely from start to finish and monitor progress of resolution • Assign accountability to Service Owners and/or first team escalated to for coordinating all activities needed to resolve tickets even if the resolution lies in another team
	Overprocessing	• Too many call options presented to users when they call the Service Desk • Too many ticket classification categories or classification schema that is needlessly complex • High volumes of incident tickets coming in • High volumes of request tickets coming in	• Reduce call management options to a low number and use more hierarchies of options versus having users sit through long lists of options • Classify tickets by service and utilize an impacted configuration item on the ticket • Investigate sources of high ticket volumes such as poorly design services, faulty hardware or poorly handled production transition • Utilize self service capabilities for commonly used requests

	Category	Areas Of Waste	What Might Be Done
	Overproduction	• Resolving the same incidents over and over without ever fixing what causes them in the first place • Producing ticket histories and databases that have classification and resolution categories that make it hard or impossible to identify which services and configuration items may need more attention	• Aggressively undertake Problem Management activities to find root causes of incidents and take actions to remove those causes • Institute improvement programs to noticeably reduce incident volumes • Classify tickets by service and utilize an impacted configuration item on the ticket • Separate incidents from requests when reporting so there is clarity on where issues may lie

Reducing Ticket Touch Points

It is not uncommon for Service Desks and IT support staff to have high number of touch points for each ticket they are dealing with. Observations have shown that it is not uncommon for a typical incident ticket to experience an average from 8 to 17 touches. The value stream diagram below depicts the typical experience of most help desks, where a ticket enters the process stream and is touched many times depending on the skill and knowledge of the support personnel.

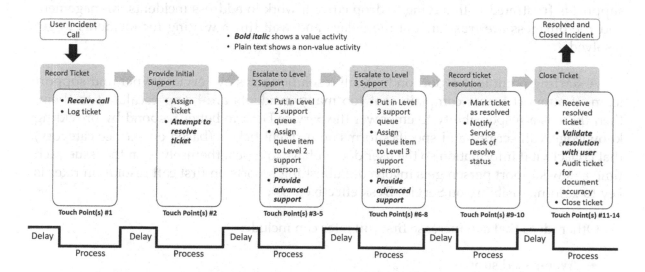

One thing that is clear from the above: first call resolution is absolutely key! You can see how many touch points and non-value activities take place once a ticket needs to be escalated. Non-value activities represent a large portion of the overall process time. The impact of that escalation is immense:

- Touch points are increased greatly when a ticket is escalated
- Support teams have to deal with unplanned labor to deal with escalated incidents
- Management and administrative follow-up is needed to make sure escalated tickets get processed in a timely manner and do not fall through the cracks
- End user delay time is greatly increased as escalated calls are queued and time is wasted waiting for a support technician to be assigned and ready
- Business satisfaction with the Service Desk and IT in general is decreased due to the delays and handoffs
- User frustration and dissatisfaction is increased
- The business may be impacted for longer periods of time waiting for resolution
- Overall unplanned labor costs rise sharply
- Projects and enhancements may be delayed due to Level2/3 resources having to drop those activities to address an incident

Therefore, a tight clear and highly prioritized focus needs to be made on resolving incidents at that first contact point. Despite this, many IT organizations still cannot articulate what their resolution rates are that indicates a lack of focus in this area. Those organizations that can still report rates that average well under 35%. Less than 50% of organizations even utilize any kind of proactive Problem Management process to reduce incidents and escalations.

Frustration, waits and delays abound throughout all of IT over this. The Service Desk is frustrated with the additional administrative work and follow-up activities. Level2/3 support is frustrated with having to drop current work to address incidents. Management and the business are frustrated at the delays and wait times waiting for incidents to get resolved.

A starting point is to report on first call resolution rates by service owner and support team. If support teams complain that too many incidents are being escalated to them, then there is a responsibility to empower the Service Desk to better respond by providing knowledge, call scripts, and specifics forms on incident tickets (based on service category) that collect vital information so the user doesn't have to repeat themselves on the issue each time a new support person gets involved. Publishing reports on first call resolution rates is key to gaining visibility on Service Desk effectiveness.

Other ideas that can increase first call rates can include:

- Web-based support
- Frequently asked questions (FAQs)
- Increasing overall call agent skills
- Job rotation and use of multi-skilled call agents
- Handling first level tickets with teams of agents that have diverse or advanced skills versus just one agent
- Restructured incentives and rewards that focus on team attainment versus individuals

Leaning Out Monitoring and Event Management

The Eight Deadly Wastes chart below (See ITSM Lean Toolkit Chapter) has been filled out for the Monitoring and Event Management. This summarizes common places where waste exists. It also provides some ideas on how you might address the waste identified.

	Category	Areas Of Waste	What Might Be Done
	Inventory	• Producing, managing and administering more alarms and alerts than what is needed	• Remove alerts that are causing "noise" • Ensure alerts are filtered properly so "noise" alerts are not being generated
	Talent	• Only monitoring basic hardware and software events because staff does not know how to monitor availability or other items for applications or services	• Use the concepts described for DevOps to get involved during application design efforts to build in monitoring capabilities versus trying to find ways to do this after the solution is ready to go live
	Waiting	• Delays between the time a critical alert is triggered to the time someone actually responds to it	• Auto-create incident tickets from critical alerts versus depending on staff to see and recognize events • Consider better communication channels for alerts such as display boards or audio alarms • Forward critical alerts to teams versus individuals

	Category	Areas Of Waste	What Might Be Done
	Motion	• Manually creating incident tickets from monitored events • Generating alerts too late such that support teams don't have enough time to properly address them • Not exposing alerts to others who may need to understand the current state of the infrastructure (e.g. Service Desk)	• Auto-create incident tickets from critical alerts • Use warning alerts for critical items followed by a later critical alert to provide support staff with enough time to react • Generate critical alerts at lower thresholds to provide support staff with enough time to react • Ensure alerts from one team are always exposed to at least one other team (e.g. Service Desk) and don't allow support teams to "hide" alerts and events
	Defects	• Sending alerts to the wrong support teams • Alerts that trigger when they are not supposed to • Implementing applications and solutions without capability for them to be monitored	• Use the concepts described for DevOps to get involved during application design efforts to build in monitoring capabilities versus trying to find ways to do this after the solution is ready to go live • Alerts that are sent to wrong support teams should be raised as an incident or request that needs to be addressed
	Transportation	• Sending alerts to teams that are not needed to take any further action	• Periodically review alert counts and whether they were used by support teams to eliminate those alerts that are no longer needed or provide little value

	Category	Areas Of Waste	What Might Be Done
	Overprocessing	• Use of way too many tools that monitor discrete parts of the infrastructure that are seldom looked at • Raising lots of monitoring "noise" events that are informational or symptomatic versus those that you really need to take action upon	• Review tools that are in place for monitoring and rationalize which ones are really needed • "Just in case" is not an excuse to keep a tool around – if it has not been used or its events not needed then consider removing it • Focus on event filtering and correlation to reduce "noise" events
	Overproduction	• Purchase of best in breed monitoring platforms when only basic functions might be needed	• Review tools that are in place for monitoring and rationalize which ones are really needed

Leaning Out Request Fulfillment

The Eight Deadly Wastes chart below (See ITSM Lean Toolkit Chapter) has been filled out for the Request Fulfillment process. This summarizes common places where waste exists. It also provides some ideas on how you might address the waste identified.

	Category	Areas Of Waste	What Might Be Done
	Inventory	• Automating requests that few or no users ever use	• Identify usage of requests on a periodic basis and do not spent efforts to automate requests that are infrequently used
	Talent	• Using manual labor to fulfill common frequent requests • High variance in processes for how requests are fulfilled (same fulfillment team may process the same kind of request in multiple ways)	• Aggressively automate requests that are frequent and common • Use automation to avoid fulfillment errors, increase fulfillment speed and enforce fulfillment processes and policies
	Waiting	• Delays associated with processing and fulfilling requests manually • Delays associated with having much more request demand than fulfillment teams can handle	• Review demand volumes and rebalance fulfillment resources as needed • Consider automating requests as a strategy to reduce need for more labor resources • Use automation to avoid fulfillment errors, increase fulfillment speed and enforce fulfillment processes and policies

	Category	Areas Of Waste	What Might Be Done
	Motion	• Entering request tickets in one system and then re-entering them in another system used by the fulfillment team	• Aggressively move to rationalize request systems such that one system is used for all requests • If multiple systems can't be avoided, automate interfaces between them to keep requests synchronized
	Defects	• Closing requests that have not be fulfilled to the user's satisfaction • Missing fulfillment service targets (SLAs) • Improperly recording requests • Improperly communicating request status to users	• Provide users with a dashboard that can highlight the status of their requests (e.g. "My Requests" dashboard which many tools now provide) • Utilize the IT Service Management system tool(s) to record and process requests • Use automation to avoid fulfillment errors, increase fulfillment speed and enforce fulfillment processes and policies • Review problematic requests with Value Stream Analysis and other process improvement tools to identify how those requests may be delivered more efficiently
	Transportation	• Improperly recording requests such that fulfillment teams have to go back to the user for more information	• Utilize scripts and specific screen forms to capture needed request information at the point the request is made

	Category	Areas Of Waste	What Might Be Done
	Overprocessing	• Initiating too many notifications to users about the status of their requests	• Eliminate use of emails or other notifications that are unnecessary • Provide users with a dashboard that can highlight the status of their requests (e.g. "My Requests" dashboard which many tools now provide)
	Overproduction	• Providing users with much more than they originally requested (over delivering)	• Review problematic requests with Value Stream Analysis and other process improvement tools to identify how those requests may be delivered more efficiently

When leaning out requests, look for ways to cut delays out of fulfillment processes. Utilize the 4 strategies described in the Lean IT Applied To ITSM chapter of this book (Leaning Out Processes) for reviewing each fulfillment process and identifying ways those can become more efficient. A key strategy is to aggressively seek out automation and self-service opportunities for frequently used requests.

The 40-40-40 Program For Problem Management

Want to pump up your Service Desk with a program that excites executives, provides great business value and greatly lowers unplanned labor costs, incident volumes and service outages? The 40-40-40 Program is a fast paced attention getting program that targets a 40% reduction in incident counts, 40% reduction in resolution times and a 40% increase in support staff skills for getting to root causes and eliminating the incidents they cause. This chapter describes how the program works and presents some examples used in a large IT organization. The approach described here can be used in any IT organization.

One of the biggest headaches in any IT organization is that of unplanned labor. This is time spent by IT executives, managers and support staff to deal with incidents and outages, rework, and recovery activities. In today's DevOps world, this is called technical debt. It carries a per hour labor price tag. This cost doesn't even include other costs such as project delays, poor customer satisfaction, penalties and fines that are triggered when everyone has to drop what their working on to deal with these unplanned issues.

The main objective of the 40-40-40 Program is to target this headache. The 3 key objectives include:

- **Reduce Incidents** - Proactively trend incidents and initiate actions to remove their underlying root causes thereby stopping incidents before users see them and reducing unplanned labor costs by 40%
- **Reduce Incident Impact** – For those incidents that can't be readily removed, reduce average outage times by 40% by initiating workarounds and resolutions and taking actions to minimize incident impact
- **Increase Skillsets** – Upgrade Service Desk and support team analysis and problem solving skills to reduce the amount of labor on these tasks by 40%. This is time that support teams spend on analyzing incidents and getting to root cause.

Here are the steps you can take to get the program going:

Step	Action
1	Ensure reporting is in place for incidents
2	Determine your baseline technical debt – labor spent on incidents
3	Agree the program with senior executive leadership
4	Train IT staff and management on problem management core concepts
5	Arm staff with Problem Management techniques that efficiently get to root cause
6	Instruct staff to proactively raise problem tickets and monitor their progress
7	Log and prioritize key activities from problem tickets to reduce incident counts and coordinate activities to resolve them or reduce their impact

Step 1 - Ensure Reporting Is In Place for Incidents

Make sure you have adequate reporting in place that can provide basic metrics – these include:

- Incident counts (ideally by service, application/device or support team)
- Incident durations – typically from ticket creation to ticket resolution
- At least 6 months to a year of ticket history

These should be present in almost any IT Incident Management system. If not, your organization is operating blindly and probably has bigger issues than could be addressed by this program.

In addition, you will also need:

- Problem Ticket logging and reporting capabilities
- Continual Service Improvement (CSI) Register for logging and prioritizing resolution activities and their progress

While the above can be found in many IT Service Management systems, you can also handle these with spreadsheets if those don't exist.

Step 2 – Determine Your Baseline Technical Debt

In this step you will baseline your current unplanned labor costs. Here is an approach (taken from a real IT organization) to do that:

A. Get the overall IT annual labor budget (e.g. $125M)
B. Get the number of IT employees (e.g. 1,100)
C. Determine the average IT burdened salary cost (A/B or $113,636)
D. Estimate average hours worked in a year for IT employees (1,832 – an industry average)
E. Calculate the IT hourly labor cost (C/D or $62)
F. Get the Incident ticket duration in hours for each incident ticket (from your reports)
G. Apply a Labor Factor (Percentage of ticket duration that incurred labor versus time the ticket was just sitting in a queue waiting – it's okay to estimate – our example used 5% for all tickets)
H. Calculate the ticket unplanned labor cost for each ticket (E-(Hourly Rate * (F-Ticket Duration) * (G-Labor Factor)))

Step 3 - Agree the Program with Senior Executive Leadership

The results from Step 2 can be put in a spreadsheet or reporting tool and presented to executive leadership for their buy-in. Here is an example of what was shown to senior executives in our example IT organization:

Ticket Category (IT Service)	# Tickets	Average Ticket Cost	Average Ticket Cost
Database Server Support	2189	$ 242	$ 27,144
Database Systems	1899	$ 589	$ 23,548
DCFS Website	17013	$ 787	$ 210,961
Desktop Printer	15278	$ 324	$ 189,447
Desktop Telephone	188986	$ 267	$ 2,343,426
DHR County Wide	524	$ 85	$ 6,498
E-Cloud Support	14378	$ 537	$ 178,287
Ecommerce	191	$ 296	$ 2,368
E-mail and Calendaring	196452	$ 454	$ 2,436,005
Enterprise Content Management (ECM) - ISSD	3564	$ 614	$ 44,194
Enterprise Geographic Information Systems (eGIS)	170	$ 264	$ 2,108
Enterprise Systems Monitoring	9085	$ 722	$ 112,654
Facilities and Energy Management Applications	501	$ 222	$ 6,212
Family Court Interagency Data Information Systems	223	$ 77	$ 2,765
Financial	11181	$ 707	$ 138,644
Hardware	206337	$ 477	$ 2,558,579
Health and Safety Ergonomics	76	$ 236	$ 942
Health Services	1055	$ 113	$ 13,082
Human Resources	2723	$ 1,407	$ 33,765
HVDI-Hosted Virtual Desktop	196326	$ 234	$ 2,434,442
Infrastructure and Asset Management	10874	$ 688	$ 134,838

Every dollar shown is wasted labor. Our example leadership did not like knowing that telephone incidents were costing them $2.3M a year, email issues $2.4M a year, etc. The target of the Program was to cut these costs by at least 40% across the board. This was what got buy-in from leadership to support the program and the areas highlighted above were to receive the most focus.

You can also highlight the unplanned labor portion of their IT budget. This is simply totaling all the annual unplanned labor costs and dividing by the IT annual labor budget. For example, if your IT organization spends $10M on labor and the unplanned labor adds up to $2M, then 20% of the IT budget is being wasted on technical debt activities – not a percentage many executives like to see!

It is important the executive leadership be visible and seen as leading this program. This will set the proper tone for staff and management support of this initiative.

Step 4 - Train IT Staff and Management on Problem Management Core Concepts

For this step, establish a series of communication events to introduce and train staff on the program and problem management best practices. These events should include:

- An overview of the 40-40-40 Program
- Training on Problem Management processes and techniques

- Staff and management roles and responsibilities for the program

Guidance and resources for Problem management processes and techniques can be found in many places throughout the internet. The ITIL 2011 Service Operation Book (Problem Management chapter) and 3rd party problem management approaches also come to mind.

Step 5 - Arm Staff with Problem Management Techniques That Efficiently Get To Root Cause

As part of training, it also helps to establish a Problem Management Toolkit as a support aid for IT staff and management. This is just an inventory of different techniques that can be used to quickly control activities and drive down to root causes.

A list of these might include techniques such as:

- Cause and Effect Diagram
- Box Plot
- Brainstorm
- Check Sheet
- Correlation Analysis
- Data Collection Plan
- Data Selection Sample
- Design Of Experiments (DOE)
- Fault Tree Analysis
- Five Whys
- Histogram
- Observation Post
- Pain Value Analysis
- Pareto Analysis
- Storyboard

All of the above plus more are documented in this book in the ITSM Lean Toolkit chapter. As a starting point, focus on the Five Whys tool. This is very simple but also very easy to use and effective. The steps to use this technique are described in that chapter.

As a guide, the table below lists the above techniques and what situations they may best be deployed in:

Problem Situation	Suggested Analysis Techniques
Complex problems where a sequence of events needs to be assembled to determine exactly what happened	• Correlation analysis • Technical observation post
Uncertainty over which problems should be addressed first	• Pain value analysis • Brainstorm
Uncertain whether a presented root cause is truly the root cause	• Five Whys
Intermittent problems that appear to come and go and cannot be recreated or repeated in a test environment	• Technical observation post • Brainstorming
Uncertainty over where to start for problems that appear to have multiple causes	• Pareto analysis • Cause and Effect Diagram • Brainstorm
Struggling to identify the exact point of failure for a problem	• Fault Tree Analysis • Failure Mode and Effects Analysis (FMEA) • Cause and Effect Diagram • Affinity mapping • Brainstorm
Uncertain where to start when trying to find root cause	• 5-Whys • Brainstorming • Affinity map

Step 6 - Instruct Staff to Proactively Raise Problem Tickets and Monitor Their Progress

At this point, have IT staff, management and support teams undertake activities to proactively identify root causes and activities to reduce incidents and their duration. Some key considerations when undertaking this effort include:

✓ Go for low-hanging fruit – don't spend lots of time identifying actions that yield little reduction – however tiny efforts and no-brainers should be noted as many of these done in aggregate might yield significant savings

✓ Focus on outcomes - every reduction opportunity proposed must provide an estimate of how many tickets will be avoided and an estimate for unplanned labor cost savings (using the approaches described in Step 2 earlier)

✓ Document the cost saving opportunities from Step 2 above. – these will be used to confirm and prioritize everyone's actions (see Step 7 – findings may show that many teams might need to be involved to implement the improvements)

✓ Recognize that root causes may not always be technical (e.g. lack of skills, training, communication, no ownership, poor vendor support may also be root causes)

Some key Program roles and activities to undertake from a program perspective can include:

Program Role	Key Program Activities
Problem Manager	• Owns the program • Trains support staff • Assists in identifying problems, root causes and action items • Coordinates cross-service issues • Coordinates how activities will be prioritized • Monitors progress on actions being implemented • Monitors support team compliance to the Program
Service Owners and Support Team Managers (Including the Service Desk)	• Reviews data for their service or support team • Identifies problems and known errors • Identifies options and actions to undertake to remove those errors
Service Manager, Continual Service Improvement Manager or Project Office	• Assists with business cases • Puts actions on CSI Register • Assists with prioritizing actions to be taken • Monitors the register to make sure actions are being implemented

Step 7 – Log, Prioritize and Implement Actions to Resolve Problems or Reduce Their Impact

A register should be maintained as each team identifies improvement actions. Actions get logged into the register along with their estimated cost saving opportunities. The Problem Manager then coordinates agreement across IT to prioritize which actions will take place. A monthly meeting is suggested to do this along with a review of progress of any actions agreed in previous meetings.

At a minimum, the CSI Register should contain the following:

- ID Number to quickly reference the action (e.g. X001)
- A brief title or description of the action (e.g. Fix Application XYZ User Lockouts)
- A detailed description (e.g. Remove duplicate active directory entries to avoid access errors on…)
- Effort estimate (e.g. 1 month, 3 months, 9 months, etc…)
- Savings Estimate (e.g. $40-60K)

The above is reviewed by the Problem Manager and key stakeholders to prioritize and identify action items to be undertaken. Those that are approved are then assigned to support teams and service owners for implementation. Reducing overall incident volumes is the key driver when prioritizing actions, so don't waste time on efforts that only address a small number of incidents.

To communicate Program activities to key stakeholders and executives, the chart below presents one way of summarizing what the Program is undertaking:

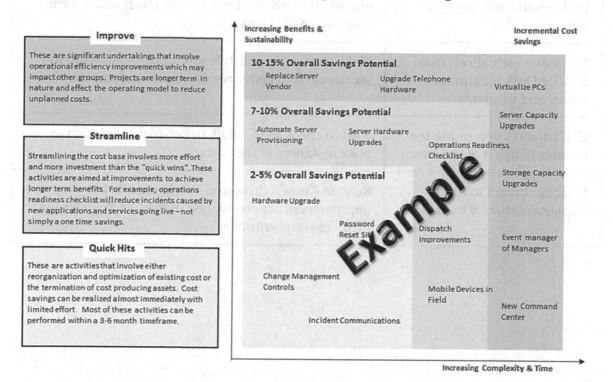

At a minimum, the Program should provide communications on a monthly basis showing business based outcomes such as lower costs and incident counts.

On an ongoing basis, the Problem Manager also monitors compliance to the Program. This can be done by looking at the incident counts for each support team or service and comparing that against things like number of problem tickets raised, total cost savings identified and implementation assignments. The bottom line is to make sure each team or service is proactively working to improve things and not just being reactive.

As a last note, the table below identifies challenges you may run into with this Program and what you might do about them:

Challenge Or Risk	Suggested Mitigation
Staff struggles to find root causes	Consider stronger use of ITSM Lean Toolkit techniques
Not enough time to proactively find problems	Time box efforts e.g. commit to 2 hours per week to focus solely on problems or assign a resource part time
Staff is unsure how Problem Processes might work	Contact Problem Management Team for guidance
Service supported is problematic and has many issues	Focus on improvements prioritizing which problems provide the greatest bang for the effort and whittle away in small chunks
Too many escalations from Service Desk for similar issues and incidents	Make sure you publish Known Errors allowing the service desk to better resolve issues independently
Can't always determine the business impact of outages	Start to check the CMDB, ticket documentation or prior instances of the issue
IT doesn't want to fund implementation activities	Rely on Known Error and Workarounds but keep improvement actions logged in the CSI Register with their cost opportunities

Chapter
11

Leaning Out Service Design

Leaning Out Service Design Tasks

With Service Design, waste is a bit different. Service Design activities themselves can be streamlined through the concepts presented earlier in this book such as Agile and DevOps. However, Service Design generally produces more cascading waste than any of the other ITSM processes. Poorly designed services might have been implemented with little waste, but their side effects produce tons of waste and unplanned costs if not done correctly. It is unfair to blame that waste on operations and delivery teams if the service was never designed properly in the first place.

The Eight Deadly Wastes chart below (See ITSM Lean Toolkit Chapter) has been filled out for Service Design tasks. This summarizes common places where waste exists. It also provides some ideas on how you might address the waste identified.

	Category	Areas Of Waste	What Might Be Done
	Inventory	• Production of SLA reports that no one reads or acts upon • Purchase of excess capacity that is not needed or before it is needed • Too many services in the Service Catalog that no one uses	• Stop producing reports that no one needs or looks at • Reduce data fields or other report items that are not actually used • Manage capacity with Container approaches (See chapter on Containerization) • Align capacity needs with business demand volumes and forecast those volumes over time • Utilize just-in-time facilities for capacity needs such as Cloud IaaS services, Outsourcing, Virtualization or Containerization capabilities • Consolidate resources with low utilization • Eliminate services from the Service Catalog that no one uses
	Talent	• Negotiating SLAs individually with each business unit • Starting SLA negotiations from a "what do you need" perspective	• Establish standard SLAs as part of a service and include them in service descriptions • Present SLAs to the business as "this is what comes with the service" as a starting point
	Waiting	• Operating with long lead times until a business can get new services • Issuing SLA, capacity and availability reports late or too long after events have occurred	• Utilize agile approaches to develop new services faster and in smaller increments • Automate production of SLA, capacity and availability reports from incident, problem and event data • Leverage incident management tool capabilities for SLA tracking and alerting to the greatest extent possible

	Category	Areas Of Waste	What Might Be Done
⇅	Motion	• Issuing custom SLA agreements that are different for each business unit • Unplanned purchases of hardware and software • Poorly presented Service Catalog such that users can't find the services they need or abandon it altogether	• Establish standard SLAs as part of a service and include them in service descriptions • Present SLAs to the business as "this is what comes with the service" as a starting point • Align capacity needs with business demand volumes and forecast those volumes over time • Utilize a Service Catalog with attractive user interfaces and service groupings so services may easily be found

	Category	Areas Of Waste	What Might Be Done
⊘	Defects	• Going live with services that are poorly designed such that IT (and the business) spend lots of unplanned labor time to deal with them • Delivering services without any SLAs or service targets • Agreeing to service targets that cannot be met by the design of the service • Establishing SLA agreements with measures that cannot be obtained • Designing and implementing SLAs that are misaligned with business objectives • Not acting on SLA breaches when they occur (for both incidents and requests) • Implementing services that carry high levels of availability risk • Providing services that are not in the IT Service Catalog or agreed to • Costs and delays related to poor supplier agreements	• Ensure services undertake architecture and design reviews to ensure they can be operated at acceptable cost and risk (see DevOps chapter) • Ensure each service has SLAs designed and built into them as a quality assurance check before those services go live • Ensure service design includes conformance to SLAs • Ensure that the business agrees to all SLA measures as well as the inputs and calculations that make them up • Ensure all SLA breaches are reported on and acted upon • Conduct thorough risk assessment of availability during design to ensure availability risks are mitigated before services go live • Institute a policy that if a service is not in the Service Catalog, then it won't be offered (unless later agreed to and placed there) • Review each supplier contract and be prepared to renegotiate terms and conditions if services and service targets are inadequate

	Category	Areas Of Waste	What Might Be Done
	Transportation	• Manually producing SLA, capacity and availability reports	• Automate production of SLA, capacity and availability reports from incident, problem and event data • Leverage incident management tool capabilities for SLA tracking and alerting to the greatest extent possible
	Overprocessing	• Issuing too many SLA agreements such that a heavy administration burden is needed to manage them	• Minimize the number of SLAs and agreements to the greatest extent possible • Utilize generalized SLA agreements that can be applied across the enterprise e.g. an SLA base agreement
	Overproduction	• Utilizing more SLA measures than the business cares about • Designing features and functions into a service that are far beyond what the business will ever need or use	• Only provide those SLAs that the business cares about • Utilize agile approaches to building services such that services are enhanced incrementally to avoid over design or over build

Defining IT Services With 6 Strategies

An IT organization that cannot clearly articulate its services is lost. It is just reacting to business needs and is operating with more complexity, waste and unplanned costs than necessary.

Most IT organizations have challenges in determining what their IT services are and how these might be presented to the business. They have already been delivering things for many years, just without any service focus or discipline. Therefore, challenges will exist in taking what is being delivered today and repackaging that into service bundles and offerings.

Why bother? After all, if IT is delivering on things today, what's the point of recasting everything into services? The answer is that the current way of delivering is not sustainable for the future. Technology and the rapid pace of business change are moving so fast. The complexity of the IT infrastructure is growing. A key purpose of casting things into services is to hide that complexity from the business. With complexity in operation, finger pointing, delays and higher delivery costs occur.

Let's take an example: an IT organization is providing banking services to customers over a mobile device through a device app, over the internet, hosted by a 3rd party provider with data services running locally on a back-end virtualized server. Do present all of this to the business as 5-6 separate capabilities? They just want the banking service. No one has accountability. The attempt of this section is to help those in IT determine, from what they already have, what services they are really providing in a manner that is consumable and acceptable by business people.

For the most part, IT can more quickly grasp their IT support services. These are described in detail in the Servicing ITSM book but will summarized later in this section. The struggle is around the IT business facing services. These are services that business users directly see and touch. Email is a business support service for this reason. Monitoring and backup of servers is not. The user implicitly needs those, but never sees those services directly.

An IT business facing service is a service that is based on the use of Information Technology to support a business service, business function or business process. Start by looking around your company. Which business activities appear to require the use of IT resources such as PCs, applications, networks or reports? Examples might include:

- Email services that support communication throughout the company
- Applications that support corporate functions such as Payroll, HR, Finance and Accounting
- Applications that support payment processing, billings or collections for a service or product that the company delivers
- Hosting of servers or websites that communicate or sell goods and services to outside customers

There are several strategies you can use to help identify what business facing IT services are being supported by the IT organization. Before getting into these strategies, here are some basic concepts around the concept of services:

- A service is simply anything of value given to a customer. As an example, if you are given a pair of shoes, you have not been given a service. If the shoes are shined, laces tied, heels repaired and placed on your feet for you, a service will have been rendered. Therefore, simply providing an IT technology, says a server for example, is not providing a service. If that server is maintained, repaired and managed, then a service has been given.

- Services should not be confused with organizations or IT units within the company. For example, a NOC (Network Operations Center) is not a service. The NOC itself could deliver services such as Monitoring, Incident Response or Event Management.

- Services come with features. These describe in lower level detail, what the customer will get with the service. Features for the Email Messaging Service, for example, might include storing and forwarding of electronic messages, distribution list management, 100MB of mailbox storage, calendaring and meeting scheduling capabilities.

- Services come with requests. These are actionable items that can be requested by the user for something the service provides. Requests for the Email Messaging Service might include "Setup a new account", "Resize a mailbox", or "Restore an email message". When designing and building a service, IT needs to get inside the head of those who will be using the service. What will they ask of the service? This means identifying all the possible types of requests that the service needs to include and ensuring the appropriate workflows and automation is in place to efficiently fulfill those requests.

- A service can be delivered through one or more IT or business units. Delivery of IT services can happen internally within the company, through an IT shared services organization or through an external third party vendor.

- Services are delivered through Delivery Channels. These simply state to the customer how they will receive the service. As an example, an Email Messaging Service may deliver electronic messages via delivery channels such as PCs, Laptops, mobile devices and tablets.

- A Customer is an entity that will consume or receive a service. Customers have specific needs and outcomes that they expect when receiving a service. If expectations are not met, low satisfaction levels will occur no matter how well IT delivers the service. A successful outcome is usually attained if customer expectations are not only met but exceeded.

- A Buyer is an entity that pays for the service. It is important to recognize the difference between the buyers and customers. It is possible to have very high customer satisfaction levels but low buyer satisfaction levels if the costs for service delivery and support are too high. It is also possible to have low customer satisfaction levels and high buyer satisfaction levels if cost savings are achieved. Be on the lookout for these two types of situations as they create many problems for IT staff and management.

- Optionally, services can be grouped into Service Lines. A Service Line is simply a logical grouping of similar or related services. It provides easier access when looking for specific services. This is not unlike a chapter in a book or a tab in a product catalog. While not required, you may find that grouping your services into categories or lines of service makes it much easier to navigate to what someone may be looking for.

Presented here are 6 strategies you might employ to determine what Business Facing services the IT organization is providing. Pull a small team together to sort through these with a series of working sessions. The team should be composed of representatives from IT operations and development units. IT service liaisons are also quite helpful as well as some representation from the business itself. Chances are you may find that no one strategy identifies all your services. Several of these strategies might be used to identify all the services.

Strategy #1 – Organization Driven

Grab your company organization chart and build groups of business facing services from that based on what IT support they are getting. Company organization charts are also helpful in that they provide clues as to what the business feels their business services really are. These would help point out business service areas such as Sales, Marketing, Finance or Manufacturing. Identified areas could then be translated into IT Business Support services such as Sales Support, Marketing Support, Finance Support and Manufacturing Support services.

The example below presents an illustration of how an organization chart may be transcribed into IT support services that are business facing. The example below is one for a University. Look at each function on the organization chart. Does it consume IT services? If so, for what purposes?

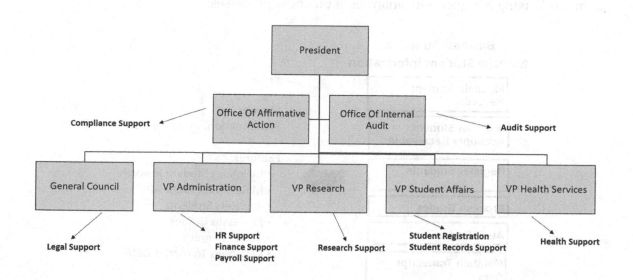

133

Strategy #2 – Business Process Driven

Identify what business processes your company runs with and turn these into business facing services. There may be a chance that the business might have undergone a business process initiative or taken a look at streamlining their business processes. If so, find stakeholders within the business units that are willing to sit down and share what business processes they operate with and which ones are using IT support.

With this approach, list each business process identified. Group like processes together. In many cases, the business may have already done this. Along with each process, identify what IT support it may be getting. Are some processes automated through IT? Are certain reports produced? Records maintained?

With this information, the grouping of business processes may become actual IT support services. Each individual process supported, report produced or record maintained will become a feature of that service. The example below illustrates how this translation might work using a higher education set of business processes.

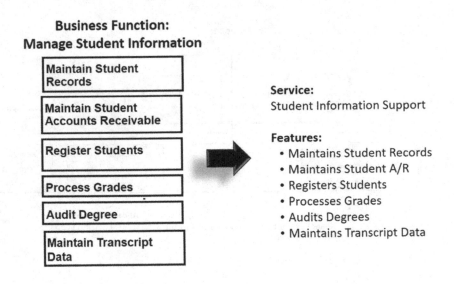

Strategy #3 – Application Driven

Go through lists of applications to build business facing services. Application inventories are a key source for driving out the IT business facing services being provided. Use working sessions to walk through the inventories line by line. For Application A, for example, what business process, service or function does it support? Develop a service name for it. For example, if Application A supports the company Sales functions, then you might call the service something like Sales Support.

Now look at the next application. Would it also fall under the Sales Support service? The criteria for this might be that the application performs similar functions or is used by the same business unit. If not, create another service that it should fall under. Repeat this step for each application you come across in your inventory. This is all illustrated by the following process flow:

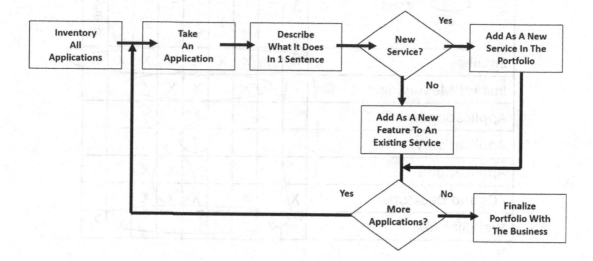

Strategy #4 – Stakeholder Driven

With this approach, identify who uses IT and group what they use it for into business facing services. The steps for this are:

1. Create a list of stakeholders (personas) that represent users of IT
2. Place each stakeholder (persona) type in a spreadsheet column
3. Meet with each stakeholder and identify what they use IT for
4. Inventory what they use IT for in rows on the spreadsheet
5. Place an X wherever a stakeholder uses a row item
6. Analyze the X's to look for groupings – these become your services

The example below takes our higher education organization and shows how this might be done:

⬭ = IT Service	Students	Parents	Faculty	Researchers	Administrator	Provost	Ombudsmen	Alumni	Government
Email	X	X	X	X	X	X	X	X	X
Instant Messaging			X		X	X	X		
Application X					X				
Application Y					X				
Application Z						X	X		
PCs and Desktops	X		X		X	X	X		
Web Site ABC		X						X	

Lots of X's in a row may indicate a service that will be provided to many stakeholders. Lots of X's in a column may indicate a service provided only to certain stakeholder types.

Once identified, you may need to translate some row items into business terms, IT services or features. In the above example, the row item Web Site ABC may be translated to an "Alumni Support Service" with a feature like "Web Portal to communicate with other Parents and Alumni".

Strategy #5 – Continuity Plan Driven

Someone else in the IT organization may have already identified what services are critical. IT Service Continuity Plans are a good source. These will indicate a more enterprise perspective of what the company sees as their services. Plans may also point out which services are considered critical to company business operations.

Strategy #6 – Steal From Professionals

It's okay to see what other IT organizations have done to get ideas. Use the web to find service descriptions that in some cases have been professionally done by others. For example, if you provide Hosting Support services to developers, go out and look at Cloud provider web sites that provide hosting support for development. See how they have presented their services. What features they tout.

As you do this, here are some other things you can try simply using the internet:

- Using your browser, type **Hosted** in front of anything you might be delivering to the business organization (e.g. "Hosted Email" "Hosted SharePoint", "Hosted HR", etc.) See what shows up and how any providers shown described their services for those items.

- Using your browser, look for IT service companies. How did they present their services? What services do they highlight? What features?

- Using your browser, look for examples of Service Catalogs that may have been posted there by other business organizations. Public Universities, State and Local Government agencies are especially good at posting their catalogs online. These may give you lots of additional ideas.

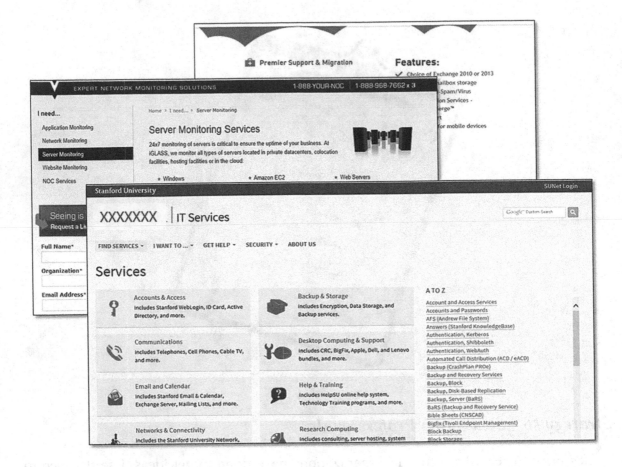

Once your analysis efforts have completed, look at the number of services that were identified. Ideally, this number should be less than 80. More than that, you may be working at too fine a level of detail. Keep in mind that the more services you define, the more overhead and administration you will create in defining, managing, operating and reporting on services in your infrastructure.

Some companies like to brag how they operate with a list that numbers thousands of services. Observations have shown that these companies typically have a long list of services that no one pays much attention to. Try to keep your list as small as reasonably possible. A list of about 40-70 services for a mid-size to large business should be generally reasonable. If your list seems overly long, take a second pass through your list with the following things you might try:

- Look for opportunities to combine or consolidate services. For example, you may have a list that shows support services for General Ledger, Accounts Receivable, and Accounts Payable. Consider combining all those services into a single Corporate Accounting Support service.

- Chances are you are mixing requests with services. Many IT organizations make the mistake of constructing Service Catalogs based on requests. Requests are part of a service. They are things that users might ask for when accessing a service. As an example, you may have requests for provisioning a server, decommissioning a server, change a server configuration, add memory to a server, etc. These are all types of requests for a Server Management support service, not multiple individual services.

What about the IT support services? These are services that are necessary to keep the business running, but are not directly consumed by business users. For example, backup and recovery support services are necessary, but the user does not see these directly as a service. At best, these services might be a feature for a business facing service ("...our features include full recovery in the event you lose your files...").

A comprehensive list of common IT support services is shown below:

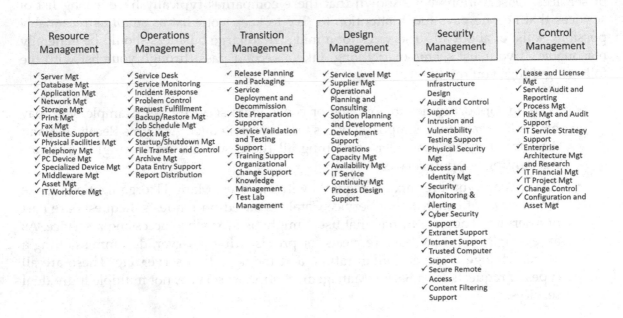

Resource Management	Operations Management	Transition Management	Design Management	Security Management	Control Management
✓ Server Mgt ✓ Database Mgt ✓ Application Mgt ✓ Network Mgt ✓ Storage Mgt ✓ Print Mgt ✓ Fax Mgt ✓ Website Support ✓ Physical Facilities Mgt ✓ Telephony Mgt ✓ PC Device Mgt ✓ Specialized Device Mgt ✓ Middleware Mgt ✓ Asset Mgt ✓ IT Workforce Mgt	✓ Service Desk ✓ Service Monitoring ✓ Incident Response ✓ Problem Control ✓ Request Fulfillment ✓ Backup/Restore Mgt ✓ Job Schedule Mgt ✓ Clock Mgt ✓ Startup/Shutdown Mgt ✓ File Transfer and Control ✓ Archive Mgt ✓ Data Entry Support ✓ Report Distribution	✓ Release Planning and Packaging ✓ Service Deployment and Decommission ✓ Site Preparation Support ✓ Service Validation and Testing Support ✓ Training Support ✓ Organizational Change Support ✓ Knowledge Management ✓ Test Lab Management	✓ Service Level Mgt ✓ Supplier Mgt ✓ Operational Planning and Consulting ✓ Solution Planning and Development ✓ Development Support Operations ✓ Capacity Mgt ✓ Availability Mgt ✓ IT Service Continuity Mgt ✓ Process Design Support	✓ Security Infrastructure Design ✓ Audit and Control Support ✓ Intrusion and Vulnerability Testing Support ✓ Physical Security Mgt ✓ Access and Identity Mgt ✓ Security Monitoring & Alerting ✓ Cyber Security Support ✓ Extranet Support ✓ Intranet Support ✓ Trusted Computer Support ✓ Secure Remote Access ✓ Content Filtering Support	✓ Lease and License Mgt ✓ Service Audit and Reporting ✓ Process Mgt ✓ Risk Mgt and Audit Support ✓ IT Service Strategy Support ✓ Enterprise Architecture Mgt and Research ✓ IT Financial Mgt ✓ IT Project Mgt ✓ Change Control ✓ Configuration and Asset Mgt

As can be seen, there are a lot of these. Do not expose these to business customers. Do not offer these individually. A best approach is to present these as bundles of support services. For example, there may be an Operations Support Service (as shown above) where all the items underneath that are features included in that service.

Implementing A High Availability Landscape

This section provides some insights for coping with the special demands of high availability. Before you implement high availability solutions, you need to first understand and assess the costs caused by service failures compared to the investment costs that will be made for high availability. This is done by:

- Estimating the costs caused by failure of the service for a specific length of time (for example, one hour), including lost revenue and the business costs of recovering from the failure.

- Estimating the costs that the business can afford to provide a reasonable level of protection against such a failure.

If it is determined that high availability solutions will be needed, plan for them as early as possible. This should go right into Service Design as soon as possible. It is easier and cheaper to build in high availability from the start than to add it in afterwards. Provisions should also be made to review availability capabilities on an ongoing basis once the service is live. Events such as changes in system configurations or business volumes might impact availability capabilities over time.

To implement a high availability landscape to support a service, take a stepwise approach that will ensure the most appropriate availability infrastructure has been chosen. Make sure that this landscape balances out cost and availability:

1. Understand the underlying architecture and configuration items that underpin the service
2. Analyze that architecture for single point of failure
3. Summarize the risks, their likelihood and impacts that could occur
4. Find the single point of failure risks that should be isolated
5. Understand the ways to isolate the single points of failure
6. Choose a setup that mitigates the single point of failure risks
7. Implement the chosen setup

To maintain a high level of availability for the service, formalized procedures must be put into place on an ongoing basis. These become more important when the underlying systems and configuration items of the service are more complex. Without such procedures, the management of availability becomes very difficult to coordinate, resulting in more chance of outages.

These procedures are shown as follows:

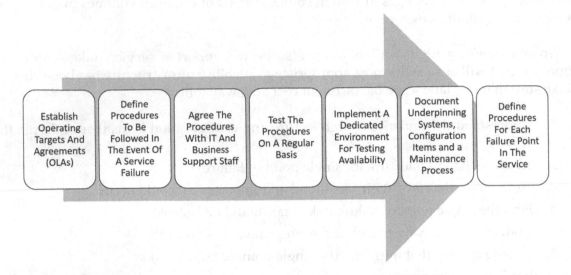

1. **Establish Operating Targets and Agreements (OLAs).** Establish operating level agreements between the support teams responsible for the system so that the required availability is guaranteed and that supporting procedures will be followed.

2. **Define Procedures To Be Followed In The Event Of A Service Failure.** Define procedures to follow in the event of failure, including escalation management and communications.

3. **Agree The Procedures With IT and Business Support Staff.** Make sure that key IT support staff approve the plans and know how to implement them.

4. **Test The Procedures On A Regular Basis.** Test procedures for handling service outages at regular intervals. Pay special attention to complex procedures for managing failures, for example, with failover mechanisms, cloud recovery interfaces or other modes of recovery. If the service is growing rapidly, adapt test procedures that are sensitive to complexity and volume, for example, database recovery.

5. **Implement A Dedicated Environment For Testing Availability.** Consider setting up a dedicated test environment that can be used for testing recovery from service failures. The test environment should match the live environment as closely as possible. In the test environment, you can simulate failures that you have identified as likely or that have critical effects on the service. Cloud solutions could play a big role with this by using those services for testing. With Cloud services, the test environment can stay synchronized with updates and changes as they are made to the live service.

6. **Document Underpinning Systems, Configuration Items and a Maintenance Process.** Document essential aspects of the system and configuration items that underpin the service. Establish procedures for updating documentation so that it always remains accurate. Establish procedures for Known Errors to the Service such that mistakes are not repeated and workarounds are ready to go in the event of a service failure.

7. **Define Procedures For Each Failure Point In The Service.** Having identified the potential risks and failure points earlier, document specific recovery procedures

for each risk/failure point. Examples might include specific steps to take if there is a database error, an application fails, hardware goes out or the network goes down.

The table below identifies needed information for a high availability setup:

Requirement	Detailed Question
Service Availability Hours	What are the normal hours of operation (that is, the period when the service is needed)
	Do the hours of operation include only the time when online users access the system or also time when batch jobs or other interfaces need access?
	What are the end users' expectations regarding uptime during normal hours of operation, for example, can they tolerate interruptions of a couple of minutes or hours?
Maximum Service Outage Duration	What is the maximum downtime before you see a minor business effect?
	What is the maximum downtime before you see a severe business impact (that is, loss of business)?
	What is the maximum downtime before your business is at risk?
	Do you have special or unusual availability requirements (that is, critical periods of a service that should not be interrupted at all or where an interruption can be tolerated for less than a couple of minutes only)?
	What kinds of failures would cause significant problems?

Requirement	Detailed Question
Service Design	Is the service solution installed on existing hardware or is the entire hardware new?
	Was the service solution planned with high availability in mind?
	Have installation options been evaluated for application and database servers?
	Are special technologies in place to support load balancing and failover?
	Are redundant network components in place?
	Are business drivers (business events that consume the service such as number of employees, widgets produced, number of users, etc.) known?
	What is the expected demand volumes for each business driver and are there peak times versus off-peak times when volumes occur?
	Are weak points and single point of failures known?
	Which components fail most frequently?
	Which components are the most difficult to replace in the event of failure?
Internal Resources	Is there a budget available to implement high availability features?
	What is the availability of qualified personnel to operate the service?
	Is the training of qualified personnel planned?
External Resources	Are support contracts and operating agreements (OLAs) in place?
	Can the system that underpins the service be supported and maintained remotely?
Environment	Are environmental or other failures likely, for example, unstable power supply in the area the business resides in?

99.X% Availability Only Angers The Business

A common practice for many years and still in place today is to publish SLAs with service targets for availability that look like 99.X%. IT does this because "that is what their toolsets will measure". The targets cite "availability", but they are really uptime measures for configuration items that can be reported on by the current toolsets.

It can't be said enough that this practice really gets the business upset. Here is how the business views those targets when published by IT:

- Most of the time they are in technical terms that the business does not understand and therefore lessens their confidence in IT capabilities

- The 99.X% target may indicate uptime for configuration items, but that does not mean the service itself is up and running providing value for the business

- Explanations for how 99.X% is calculated tend to be tortuous, complex and confusing

- No one wants to pay for 99.X% availability – would you buy a car that only works 99.X% of the time?

- A single major outage occurs that causes great stress on the business yet IT reports that they met their 99.X% target because the outage wasn't long enough

Here is an interesting effect that occurs all too often when delivering services:

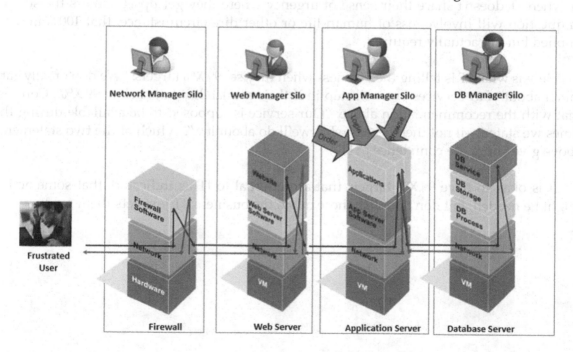

Here IT is operating in engineering silos (e.g. Firewall, Database, etc.). Each is providing high levels of availability. All these silos underpin a service that a user is getting. So why the frustration? Answer: the combined effect of everyone delivering at 99.9% is really much lower! Availability is from the user perspective is not 99.9% - it is 99.9% x 99.9% x 99.9% x etc.

A result that is much lower. The reason? Not all silos have an outage on the same day at the same time. On Monday the database goes out. Tuesday the database is up but the Firewall is having problems. Wednesday the Application Server goes down.

The user is experiencing all of these, but IT only sees them individually. This is where the big disconnect happens. The user is out there complaining that they constantly have availability issues with their service. IT responds by saying that they met all their availability targets and is delivering wonderful service. Doesn't the business understand the great job IT is doing for them?

The suggestion here is to stop publishing service targets on availability in terms like 99.X%! This serves no purpose. It isolates IT from the business they serve. So here is a suggestion:

Focus on unavailability by publishing targets in these simple terms:

Our service is available Mondays through Fridays from 9am to 5pm (for example).

The IT skeptics may be concerned with the above. "We can't deliver 100% availability. That requires sophisticated load balancers, redundancy and oversight that we can't afford". Here is a little secret: the business is sophisticated enough to know that things go wrong in IT. They want to know that IT is in top of things and will be have their backs covered if things go south. It's when things happen over and over, IT doesn't appear to be listening or when IT doesn't share their sense of urgency where they get upset. Unless the service in question will involve loss of human life or other dire circumstance, that 100% may be implied but not actually required.

Here is what IT is telling the business when they set 99.X% targets: "We don't really care much about your services but will step in if their availability falls below 99.X%". Contrast that with the recommendation above: "Our service is supposed to be available during the times we stated – if not then here is what we'll do about it…". Which of the two statements above give you more confidence in IT?

It is okay to have 99.X% targets that are internal to IT as indicators that some action might be needed, but don't publish these out to the business. IT just gets them mad!

Capacity Modeling And Forecasting Basics

The ability to model future capacity is critical to prevent waste and costs related to unplanned purchases of hardware and software or service outages and slowdowns. This aspect of IT Service Management is a bit unknown. This section provides some help.

There are some items of information that need to be gathered before modeling efforts can start. These are:

- Information on service workloads and the business driver(s) that will consume them (e.g. Manufacturing Control Line Support Service will have Requests For Product Information)
- Time period when expected business volumes will occur (e.g. expect 1,000 requests per hour in Q3 and 1,200 requests per hour in Q4)
- Estimate of time in the system that underpins the service for each request or transaction type (e.g. each request spends 0.3 seconds in the system).

With this basic information, there are several ways to model for the capacity needed to operate. The table below presents a list of common modeling techniques and when you might use them:

Simplicity Level	Accuracy Level	Modeling Technique	Effort Level	Description
1	30-50%	Back-Of-The-Napkin	Low	Quick approach where you may multiply planned transaction volumes x estimated resource usage per transaction to arrive at a high estimate of capacity needed.
2	40-60%	Analytical	Low	Also quick. Usually involves using a spreadsheet to list resources, time at each resource per transaction and look for high utilizations and bottlenecks. Can model changes in volumes or what happens if less time is needed at each resource.

Simplicity Level	Accuracy Level	Modeling Technique	Effort Level	Description
3	60-70%	Queuing Theory	Moderate	Similar to the Analytical approach but applies queueing formulas to predict user response times for each transaction. The more utilized resources are, the higher user response times will go. Impact on response times can be seen by changing resource speeds or time in the system. Also allows you to see which components may become bottlenecks as demand volumes rise. Excellent for steady state conditions, not so good if business volumes change erratically.
4	70-75%	Stochastic Simulation Modeling	Moderate To High	Simulates the live environment by representing configuration items, volumes and loads mathematically. Much more complex than Analytical modeling, it is highly recommended to utilize vendor modeling tools that hide the complex formulas through modeling languages. Has added benefits in that you can see where in the underlying system bottlenecks may exist at detailed levels.

Simplicity Level	Accuracy Level	Modeling Technique	Effort Level	Description
5	60-70%	Industry Benchmarking	Moderate	Involves research and information on industry experience with similar service solutions, the volumes they handle and how the underlying systems were sized to deal with those volumes. Not a bad approach as it is based on actual experience. Not so good if the target environment is different than what was used for the benchmark although some assumptions could be applied.
6	70-80%	Synthetic Transactions	Moderate To High	This involves development staff wherein special transactions are developed that traverse the system on a regular basis that drop timing and log information as they execute. This allows you to see real-time performance of the system in a live state. Volumes can be simulated by increasing the volume of the transactions to observe their effect and impact. Not a waste of time for development as this also has the added benefit of gauging true end-to-end response times as the user sees them.

Simplicity Level	Accuracy Level	Modeling Technique	Effort Level	Description
7	85-95%	Full Benchmark	High to Very High	This involves a complete build of the live system in a test environment, having real users (or simulated ones if load testing software is used) execute transactions and observing the results. The most accurate means for testing performance and capacity. It is also expensive in that live people are involved, production environment has to be simulated and a means in place to monitor and record results. Use of Cloud facilities for this might be helpful.

For our modeling example we will take an approach that falls around Simplicity Level 3. That is the use of basic queueing algorithms for capacity modeling. This is a basic approach but provides some benefits in sizing and predicting service performance.

The methodology is as follows:

1. Calculate service utilization
2. Calculate Wait Time
3. Calculate user time in the service (response time)

Let's look at an example:

1. Calculate service utilization

From 9am to 10am (1 hour), 100 users logon to access Email services. When they logon they use the Email service for about 10 minutes or 0.166 hours. With this information we can now calculate utilization of the Email service as:

Service Time Per User (0.166 Hours) x Arrival Rate Per Hour (100 users)

Service Period (1 Hour)

Or 16.6% utilization rate for the Email service.

2. Calculate Wait Time

Wait time is calculated as (Service Time / Utilization) / (1 – Utilization). Therefore:

Service Time Per User (0.166 Hours) * Utilization (16.6% or 0.166)

----

1 – Utilization (16.6% or 0.166)

Email users will wait 0.033 hours (1.98 minutes or 118 seconds) to get into the Email system.

3. Calculate user time in the service (response time)

Response time per user is then calculated as Wait Time + Service Time. Therefore:

Wait Time Per User (0.033 Hours) + Service Time Per User (0.166 Hours)

Email users are in the system for 0.199 Hours.

The above basic formulas can be applied in a spreadsheet where you can model and forecast the impact of changes to demand volumes, use of faster configuration items or changes in service times. A spreadsheet example for doing this might look like the following:

```
Utilization Calculation:

        Service Time (Secs):      2.33
        Interval (Secs):          3600
        Arrival Rate/Interval     1,000

                Utilization:          64.72%


Calculating Wait Times:

        Service Time        Utilization        Wait Time        Response Time
           2.33               78.5%             8.5123             10.8423
           2.33               80.0%             9.3200             11.6500
           2.33               99.0%           230.6700            233.0000
           2.33               10.0%             0.2589              2.5889
           2.33               50.0%             2.3300              4.6600
```

With the above, all the parameters under the Utilization Calculation can be modified as needed. The Utilization result will change based on the parameters used. Under the Calculating Wait Times section, Service Time, Wait Time and Response Time are calculated all based on the resulting Utilization. In the example above, the first line item matches the parameters given in the Utilization Calculation. Other line items have the Utilization value manually changed just to model the impact on response times.

In looking at this and based on the parameters entered, users are waiting a full 8.5 seconds to get into the system. If utilization increases to 99%, then wait time increases to 230.6 seconds. If it drops to 50%, then then wait times drop to only 4.6 seconds.

What might impact utilization to show such changes?

- Fewer or more users in the service (arrivals)
- Faster servers such that Service Time is less than that originally modeled
- Better designed system such that Service Time is less than that originally modeled
- Adding more servers that can handle user demand such that Service Time can be divided by the number of servers being added

There is only one rule around using the formulas presented here. Any time the Utilization becomes 100% or greater, the results are negated. In such a service, everyone would be waiting and never getting in. If this shows up in your model, then you would need to apply an assumption such as a faster server or more servers or less Service Time to get the utilizations below 100%.

Using Cloud for High Velocity IT Service Continuity

Hot sites/cold sites are a thing of the past. Data centers can now easily be replicated at multiple sites and instantly recovered. Traditional disaster recovery with its hot sites, cold sites, etc. is dying – and good riddance! In a high velocity ITSM world, handling of major business outages can be done by orchestrating and automating replication of on-premises physical servers and virtual machines to a Cloud service or to a secondary datacenter. The diagram below illustrates one approach for how this might work:

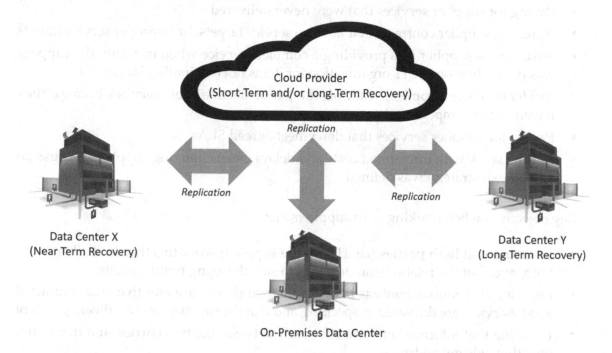

With the above, a main data center can be replicated to through the Cloud into another data center for recovery purposes. If needed, the Cloud provider themselves could also offer replication to use Cloud facilities as a recovery facility. Replication can occur at almost any time interval you choose. For example, you may want to replicate change to the alternative sites every 5 minutes, every hour, once per day or even in near real time if desired.

Use of this kind of an approach is not a complete replacement of traditional IT Service Continuity approaches. The disaster/recovery plan still needs to take people into account such as roles and responsibilities. Training and awareness in the event of a major business outage still needs to take place. Transportation of people to alternative sites may need to happen. Recovery processes still need to be managed. Provisions for software licensing at recovery sites and access still needs to maintained.

Supplier Management Is Now Critical

In a world of high velocity service management, services are being provided from many suppliers, not just the internal IT organization. Although IT is ultimately accountable for all services being delivered, suppliers are the lifeblood behind IT that keeps services operating.

As a result, the practice of Supplier Management has now become critical. Whether fixing workstations, developing a new service, taking first line Service Desk calls or managing IT infrastructure, suppliers need to be managed carefully.

Lack of attention in this area can create many operating risks such as:

- Longer service outage times due to finger pointing between IT and its suppliers
- Longer service outage times related to slow response from suppliers
- Paying for supplier services that were never delivered
- Agreeing supplier contracts that have no service targets, or improper service targets
- Assuming a supplier was providing a complete service when in reality the supplier was depending on the IT organization for items not originally planned for
- Incidents where suppliers walk off the job or decline their services because they haven't been compensated accurately
- Paying for supplier services that don't meet agreed SLAs
- Getting stuck with unplanned costs and delays when changing suppliers because no agreed exit strategy was defined

Key objectives when working with suppliers are:

- Ensuring that both parties (i.e. IT and the supplier) work together to the benefit of both, and that the relationship develops to suit changing requirements
- Ensuring that routine contacts between the two parties are effective, that contracted goods/services are delivered as specified, and that the supplier receives timely payment
- Ensuring that information flows effectively between the two parties, and that issues on either side get addressed
- Ensuring that any changes in requirement are defined and passed to the supplier, by interfacing with the normal Procurement processes

Having a Supplier Manager role is key. Every supplier used by IT should be assigned to a Supplier Manager that can serve as a single point of contact for that supplier into the IT organization. Key responsibilities for this role include:

- Taking ownership of the relationship between IT and the supplier
- Defining key players (commercial, technical, business) in the relationship, including escalation points
- Ensuring that supply agreements are appropriately defined and documented
- Ensuring that supply agreements include success criteria and measurements
- Ensuring supplier SLAs are aligned with business service delivery commitments
- Ensuring existing procedures are effective, and that staff involved in routine contact with the supplier are aware of their responsibilities
- Reviewing supplier performance against agreed metrics, and coordinating the resolution of issues that might arise
- Reviewing supplier status and ensuring any changes are captured and acted upon

- Understanding the supplier's market position and drivers, and being prepared to act to resolve issues on their behalf (e.g. delays in payment of invoices)
- Coordinating requirements for change, and maintaining a high-level plan of relevant activities
- Handling supplier cancellation in such a way as not to negatively impact IT or its customers

The Supplier Manager should maintain a file of records on each supplier. Items in this file can include:

- Supplier contact details, including escalation path
- Copies of contract papers
- Purchase orders and invoices
- Relevant correspondence
- Details of any measurements of supplier performance
- Minutes of review meetings
- Historical and forecast spend
- Issues pertaining to the relationship

A general process for managing suppliers is presented below:

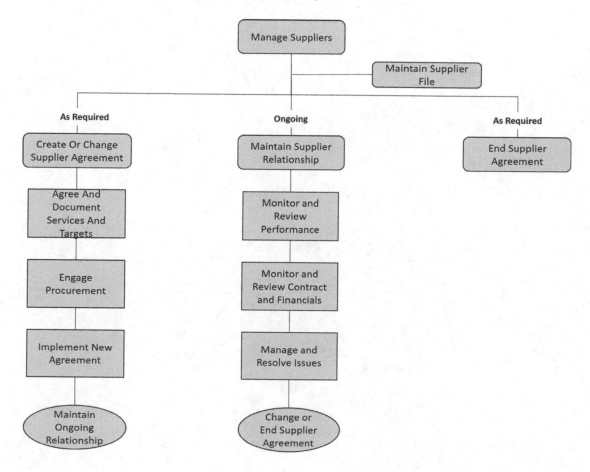

Chapter
12

Leaning Out Service Strategy

The Danger Of Operating In Engineering Silos

There is no business value in IT until the point a service is actually delivered. Yet IT typically organizes itself by engineering capability with no one accountable for a service. This means that senior leadership is hoping that each engineering silo will cooperate with other silos and work hand in hand to give the business what it needs. This approach fails miserably in many IT organizations. Why is this so?

Many IT organizations may look something like this:

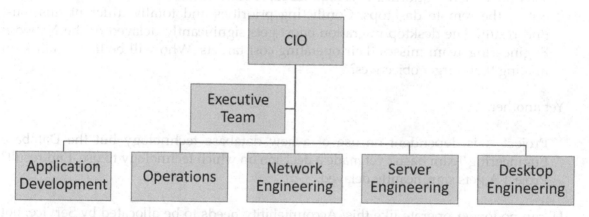

This is organization by engineering capability. Virtually no one owns a service. Where are Email? Manufacturing Control? Accounting? Human Resource Support? They are logical entities supported by the organization as shown above. Each engineering silo is accountable for a piece of the technology (or support and operations) needed to support those services. Yet no one is fully accountable from the end user of business perspective.

Service integration is like water. Therefore, it flows upward and outward. With the above, since there is no accountability within the support organization, the CIO and/or executive team is acting as service integrators whether they realize it or not. Symptomatic of this is the CIO who constantly complains that "IT can't seem to work together", or, "why do I have to call so many people in IT to get things done?" The answer is that the CIO is the service integrator.

What happens if the CIO declines to act in this role? Service integration then flows outward to the business units. Now it is business unit directors who are pushing on the CIO and IT management to get things done. "IT can't seem to get its act together", or, "why do we have to call so many people in IT before something gets done?" they will say.

Without accountability, and from a Lean perspective, waste and delays rapidly build up. Here are some examples of what typically happens:

A development team wants to finish Project A except that the project is dependent on 2 infrastructure projects as well as Project B and Project C. Each of these are owned by different teams. Who sets the priorities? Project A is rewarded on getting their code into production on time. Projects B and C are operating with different timelines. The infrastructure teams are focused on stability – not change. Each team has its own priorities and set of goals. The end result? Everything slows down.

Here is another:

The Network Engineering Team is missioned to reduce network costs. They remove site servers and other networking infrastructure to accomplish the bottom line cost reduction. At the same time, the Desktop Engineering team is moving to a Cloud-based set of desktop technologies and needs to upgrade desktop hardware and software to new platforms. This requires more bandwidth to handle pushes of images out to the remote desktops. Conflicting priorities and totally different missions. End result? The desktop migration effort gets significantly delayed or the Network Engineering Team misses their operating cost targets. Who will be first to blink on making their target objectives?

Yet another:

Project A is dependent on use of a new database technology but the Database Engineering Team hasn't yet made a decision on which technology to use. End result? Project A gets significantly delayed.

IT can no longer operate like this. Accountability needs to be allocated by Service, not engineering technology. Funding decisions should be made through a portfolio of services such that the Service Owner is accountable for the funding stream allocated to their service,

At a very minimum, the following should be in place:

- IT has an agreed portfolio of services that identify what they are providing to the business
- Service Owners have been assigned to be accountable for each service in the portfolio
- IT budgeting is done by service

- Service Owners have the highest level accountability for the quality of their service and managing funds allocated to that service

- Service Owners have a direct line to the CIO or executive team and do not reside within an engineering silo in the IT organization

- Service Owners work across the engineering silos to coordinate development, support and management of the services they own

- A governing council is in place at the executive level to straighten out any conflicts that may occur between Service Owners

With service ownership, decision making and authority is aligned to the services that the business expects to receive in order to get value from IT. This is how you "align IT to the business". Ownership has to exist formally in the IT organization with direct report to executive teams to make this happen (See Organizing ITSM – ISBN: 978-1-4907-6270-8 for how to make this happen in your IT organization).

The bottom line from a Lean perspective: not organizing as a service provider can result in higher costs and introduces delays, finger pointing and all sorts of other unwanted issues.

Five Steps To IT/Business Alignment

The role of IT is rapidly changing from engineer-to-order to service integration. What IT traditionally engineered, built, owned and operated can now be bought from many sources more easily without inheriting the specific risks of ownership, support, building and managing an operating infrastructure. Underpinning all of this is again the key point: there is no IT value to the business until the point a service is received. So if this is the case, the following needs to be in place:

- IT providers need to know clearly what services they deliver and bundle these for business consumption

- IT needs to know the overall and unit costs for delivering such services

- IT needs to understand how its services are consumed by the business (demand) and how this will look in the future

To manage all of the above, an IT Service Portfolio needs to identify each service, its costs and demand. The IT strategy becomes one of investment in IT services. Do you add new services? Build or Buy? Remove some services? Enhance some services? How much of the portfolio will be maintenance versus new? This is the essence of IT alignment. Provision investments in services in accordance with the business strategy. The IT strategy is therefore shown as a portfolio of investments, not a roster of agreed projects. When you can see costs by service, wonderful things start to happen.

IT Service Portfolio					
	Salaries	Training	Network	Servers	Etc...
IT Service 1	$99,000	$99,000	$99,000	$99,000	$99,000
IT Service 2	$99,000	$99,000	$99,000	$99,000	$99,000
IT Service 3	$99,000	$99,000	$99,000	$99,000	$99,000
IT Service 4	$99,000	$99,000	$99,000	$99,000	$99,000
IT Service 5	$99,000	$99,000	$99,000	$99,000	$99,000

Service view of costs results in hidden savings by uncovering actual service value delivered to the business

Typical internal way IT looks for costs/savings (by asset or technology)

IT costs are typically viewed in ways that do not give the business an understanding of what they are buying. Most IT organizations will take an "asset" based view of their costs (the columns in the above diagram). This merely provides the business with an accounting for what is being spent, but leaves the business (as well as IT) blind as to how these costs are being consumed and whether that consumption is even valid.

Full transparency to the business requires that costs must be seen across their value chain. This means that CIOs and other executives must be able to articulate the services they run, their costs and how the business is consuming those services. Once visible, both IT and the business begin to see optimization opportunities that were previously hidden. Here are some examples from companies that have employed this approach:

- The senior VP of a real estate company that was unaware significant IT costs were being incurred for a number of common property management functions. The quote: "if I knew IT was spending this much to provide this service I would have offloaded it to simple spreadsheets years ago..."

- A very large financial credit card processing company that discovered several services not critical to the business was consuming large amounts of resources. This resulted in immediate realized savings of over $60M.

- A large state agency that saw an immediate $4.5M in savings by taking a service view of their outsourcing costs, renegotiated their contract and plowed the savings back into other IT provided services deemed more critical to the business.

- A large federal agency that gained a $900M negotiating position with their outsourcer once it was recognized that the service value of the IT assets that supplier was providing was much less than what the supplier was touting (e.g. found myriads of service assets they were being charged for but not in the value chain for the services being delivered).

There are 5 Steps that can be taken by the IT organization effect this alignment and provide quick tactical means to provide the cost transparency described above. These steps can be done within 3-4 months for an average to large IT organization. 1-2 months if the organization is smaller. The outcomes will position senior IT leadership such that they can articulate their services, costs and demand for how their services are being used. These steps are shown below:

Step	Action	Outcome
1	Identify the portfolio of IT services	IT can communicate the services they provide to the business in business terms and what consumes those services
2	Map the IT infrastructure to that portfolio	IT can now relate the IT assets and infrastructure as a "bill of materials" for each service
3	Develop the service cost models	IT can now communicate the costs for each service
4	Assess the service delivery capabilities	IT has a solid handle around what service delivery capabilities they have and any significant gaps in those capabilities
5	Optimize IT service delivery and costs	IT now has a strategy and business plan to optimize costs and improve service quality that is aligned and presented in business terms

Step 1: Building The Service Portfolio

In this step, a portfolio of all current IT services used to support the business is developed. This is not as simple as it sounds. Business people understand services from a business perspective, but not an IT perspective. IT people will understand technologies and platforms, but not necessarily understand how these support the business. The following approach may be helpful in identifying what IT services are being delivered:

1. Inventory a list of the business functions that the business itself is operating with. Organization Charts can help identify these. Examples might include Payroll, HR, Sales, Accounting, Marketing, and Legal.

2. Link applications to those business functions by collecting lists of applications and categorizing them to their appropriate business function. For example, the application named PRISM-GL supports the Accounting business function. The application PRISM-AP also supports the accounting function. The application BL009XYZ supports the Marketing function. Should an application not fit into any of the functions previously on the list, create an additional business function and add it to the list.

3. Develop a brief one sentence summary of what each application does. As an example, a summary of PRISM-GL might be "Provides automated management of general ledger entries and accounts". PRISM-AP might be "Provides automated reporting and management of payables". BL009XYZ might be "Provides support for marketing lists and canvas-based promotional programs".

4. Inventory the "business facing" IT services and features. Take the business function list and add the word "Support" to each function. Then create a list of features for each service on the list by adding the one sentence summaries previously developed for each application that was linked to the business function. For example, the business function called "Accounting" now becomes a business facing IT service called "Accounting Support". The features for that service would be "Provides automated management of general ledger entries and accounts" and "Provides automated reporting and management of payables".

5. Supplement the list of "business facing" IT services with the IT "supporting services" that might underpin these. Examples of these can include IT services such as Incident Support, Backup/Restore Support, Job Scheduling Support, Monitoring, Application Maintenance, Break-Fix Support, etc. Since many of these are common to most IT organizations, a comprehensive list of IT supporting services and their features can be obtained separately from the author.

6. Identify business drivers that consume each service. The driver is a business element or business event that causes the usage of the service to go up or down. Examples of drivers might be elements such as number of employees, number of sales, number of customers, number of goods manufactured or number of loans processed. Considerations for identifying drivers are:

7. They must be in business (not technical) terms

8. Each service must have at least one driver but can have multiple drivers

9. Capacity and financial management staff may be helpful in identifying drivers

10. Driver volumes can be obtained from somewhere in the organization, e.g. 15,000 employees, 4,500 sales orders, 4 million widgets manufactured, etc.

11. Link IT projects with the services. Projects should be treated as one time activities to create, modify or remove a service. Therefore, identify any IT projects that may be in progress and link these with the services that they are addressing.

At this point, you have assembled a basic service portfolio that identifies:

- The IT services being delivered
- The key features provided by each IT service
- An indication as to whether each service is an IT business facing service or an IT supporting service
- A mapping of your application assets with each IT service that they underpin
- Key business drivers that consume each service
- Any projects that are associated with each service

Other considerations when building the portfolio are:

- Try to keep the list no larger than 60-80 services (if larger, you may be identifying services at too detailed a level)

- IT Service Continuity (Disaster/Recovery) plans can also be another source for identifying services as these may have already documented vital IT business functions

- Do not create separate services for desktops, mobile devices, or laptops – recognize that these are delivery channels for how those services are delivered

- Do not create separate services for different technology platforms as these can also be considered delivery channels or products – for example, you can have a single technical management support service that covers mainframes, servers, operating systems, etc.

- Services should be independent of organizational structure – you can have a service that serves multiple customers e.g. business units or departments

Step 2: Mapping Infrastructure To Services

The goal of this step is to create an underlying "bill of materials", made up of infrastructure assets, for each service identified in the previous step. You can undertake this exercise in extreme detail which might take more time, or do it with broad categories of assets to get results much faster. An approach for accomplishing this is illustrated using a basic spreadsheet example.

The first task is to lay out a spreadsheet as shown below:

Services / Assets	Service Allocations				
	Manufacturing Support	Email Support	HR Support	Etc.	Control Total
UNIX Server SaPAPI					
UNIX Server SAPDev					
Oracle DB Licenses					
AIX V6.2 OS Software					
SAP Maintenance					
Bangalore Service Desk					
Building Rental					
Facilities Accommodation					
Phoenix Development Staff					
Etc.					

With this, the services identified in Step 1 are placed across in columns. Assets (e.g. PC Server XYZ) or groups of assets (e.g. Location XYZ Servers) are placed in rows. It is okay if the level of detail for the supporting components is not overly detailed. For example, you can list each supporting server individually, or simply group them (e.g. Server Farm XYZ). Note that non-technical service assets are also listed which can include people, organizations, or support vendors. The general guiding principle is to list those service assets for which costs can be easy to identify.

Now identify the relationships between the components and the services they support. This can be done by placing an X in each row/column intersection where a relationship exists. Note that it is not unusual to find that components may support multiple services. The resulting spreadsheet to show this now looks like the following:

Services / Assets	Service Allocations				
	Manufacturing Support	Email Support	HR Support	Etc.	Control Total
UNIX Server SaPAPI	X			...	
UNIX Server SAPDev	X			...	
Oracle DB Licenses	X	X	X	...	
AIX V6.2 OS Software	X		X	...	
SAP Maintenance	X			...	
Bangalore Service Desk	X	X	X	...	
Building Rental	X	X	X	...	
Facilities Accommodation	X	X	X	...	
Phoenix Development Staff	X		X	...	
Etc.	...	...	...		

Although we've just started on this, note the value received so far: we have aligned the infrastructure with the services that are being supported. Already this provides a resource for helping to troubleshoot issues, identify what services are impacted by asset operating failures and assess impact of proposed changes on services based on what assets are being touched.

Next, identify how each component is consumed by each service that it supports. This can be done by replacing the X in each row/column with a percentage. The percentage represents how much of that component is used to support the service listed in the column header. Our spreadsheet now looks like the following:

Services / Assets	Service Allocations				
	Manufacturing Support	Email Support	HR Support	Etc.	Control Total
UNIX Server SaPAPI	100%	0%	0%	...	100%
UNIX Server SAPDev	100%	0%	0%	...	100%
Oracle DB Licenses	66%	20%	14%	...	100%
AIX V6.2 OS Software	22%	0%	34%	...	100%
SAP Maintenance	100%	0%	0%	...	100%
Bangalore Service Desk	18%	22%	12%	...	100%
Building Rental	8%	2%	2%	...	100%
Facilities Accommodation	8%	2%	2%	...	100%
Phoenix Development Staff	50%	0%	50%	...	100%
Etc.	...	...	...	...	100%

Identifying the percentages is part science and part general assumption. In some cases, the answers are easy. If the component is dedicated to a service, then the X is replaced with a 100%. If the component is shared across several services, then the percentage of consumption for each service needs to be determined. In the latter case, reasonable assumptions, capacity and labor reports or other means can be used to determine the allocations as long as there is general agreement with whatever technique was used. As an example, in the above, Oracle DB Licenses were allocated by how many employees work in Manufacturing, Email and HR Support. Note that the Control Total column is used to ensure that 100% of the asset has been accounted for. It represents a sum of all percentages across the row for each asset.

Step 3: Developing Service Cost Models

The goal of this step is to identify the current costs for delivering each service and the unit costs that drive each service. A suggested approach for this is as follows:

1. Gather all known cost information and assemble it in one place where it can be easily obtained and referenced. This involves collecting all the relevant IT financial documentation and existing budgets, cost pools and allocations. These may include items such as:

    *   IT budgets
    *   Asset costs
    *   Costs by cost pool
    *   Capital budgets
    *   Fully burdened personnel costs
    *   Project costs
    *   Indirect costs
    *   Costs for 3rd party vendor services
    *   Chargeback revenue
    *   Depreciations
    *   Cost forecasts

Populate the spreadsheet with allocation of costs to each service. Take the cost of each service asset and apportion it by the percentages in the spreadsheet converting them to dollars as shown in the following diagram:

Services \ Assets	Service Allocations				
	Manufacturing Support	Email Support	HR Support	Etc.	Control Total
UNIX Server SaPAPI	$140,000	$0	$0	...	$140,000
UNIX Server SAPDev	$140,000	$0	$0	...	$140,000
Oracle DB Licenses	$118,800	$36,000	$26,200	...	$180,000
AIX V6.2 OS Software	$134,200	$0	$140,000	...	$610,000
SAP Maintenance	$60,000	$0	$0	...	$300,000
Bangalore Service Desk	$22,446	$140,000	$140,000	...	$2,420,000
Building Rental	$40,000	$140,000	$140,000	...	$8,500,000
Facilities Accommodation	$8,816	$2,500	$2,500	...	$100,000
Phoenix Development Staff	$1,342,800	$0	$432,000	...	$2,380,000
Etc.	...	...	...	...	...
Totals:	$2,980,000	$2,980,000	$2,980,000	$2,980,000	$18,987,600

At this point you have a solid understanding of costs associated with each service. There is just one key item missing: Projects! Add in project costs for each service by identifying costs for each project and adding that cost to the service that the project is associated with.

Now calculate the unit costs for each service by taking the business drivers for each service and dividing their volume into the total cost for each service. As an example, look at the HR Support service in the diagram If we have determined that the driver volume for this service is 10,000 employees, and the total cost of the service is $2,980,000, then the IT unit cost for the HR Support service is $298 for each employee.

By the end of this third step, we have developed extremely valuable information for the IT leadership. For senior executives we have now identified:

- The services that IT is delivering to the business
- The costs for each service being delivered
- The demand and unit costs that consume each service
- The remaining steps will now focus on how to use this information to drive IT strategy.

Step 4: Assessing Current Service Capabilities

The goal of this step is to conduct a baseline assessment of the services and service delivery capabilities that exist currently in the IT organization. Use the costs developed in Step 3 as a general guide for where to focus. For example, if unit costs for one service are noticeably high, what is causing that?

167

The focus of this assessment should include:

Assessment Focus Area	Findings To Look For
Service Delivery (ITSM) Processes	ITSM process maturity, process inefficiencies, process issues, missing or problematic processes
Service Delivery Technologies	Redundant management tools, missing management tools, tools and platforms not supported, tools and platforms that may be experiencing failures, tools unused or not providing value
Service Delivery Organization	Whether roles and responsibilities are in place, whether skills are adequate, organization alignment
Service Delivery Governance	Level of operating standards, IT reporting, how new services are requested and approved, service and operating metrics, service improvement practices
Quality Of The Services Being Delivered	Business satisfaction with each service, service availability, service issues that may exist

It is highly recommended that assessment activities be conducted by a product neutral outside third party supplier if at all possible. This provides an unbiased view of the delivery capabilities. Too often, attempts to conduct assessments by the IT organization itself results in skewed findings that may be manipulated for political or other reasons. If the assessment is to be done internally, try to remove barriers that may get in the way of identifying honest findings.

At a minimum, the output of the assessment activities should yield:

- An inventory of findings and observations
- An inventory of key issues and deficiencies sorted by level of impact to the IT organization and business
- An inventory of recommendations to address key issues identified

The output results should be discussed and evaluated with the IT organization and fed into Continual Service Improvement. As with any Portfolio management effort, get a consensus across IT and the business as to what issues should be addressed first, second third, etc.

Step 5: Optimize IT Service Delivery and Costs

The goal of this step is to identify the IT strategy that will be undertaken to improve the quality of the IT services being delivered optimizing and aligning their delivery costs. This can be done by first identifying business goals and targets, ranking the services provided and then applying a technique called Lens Analysis to look for improvement areas. Identified improvement tasks will then be grouped into an inventory of desired projects. The overall approach to accomplish this is summarized as follows:

1. Gather desired business goals and priorities. These will be used as input and benchmarks for identifying and prioritizing improvement areas. It is not enough for IT to simply identify an area that could be improved. There needs to be a match against what the business is really looking for. Without this, IT will be funding efforts and projects that may not be aligned with business goals and priorities. Key inputs for identifying business goals and targets may come from items such as:

   - Published business goals
   - Business scorecards with targets
   - Prioritized project portfolios
   - Service agreements
   - Business Continuity Plans (for vital business functions)
   - IT goals and strategies already agreed to by the business

2. Rank each service in the IT Service Portfolio to make sure that both IT and the business fully understand how services are positioned from a value perspective. This will be important when trying to select service strategies. One approach for doing this might be to put services into a quadrant like that in the right hand side of the figure below:

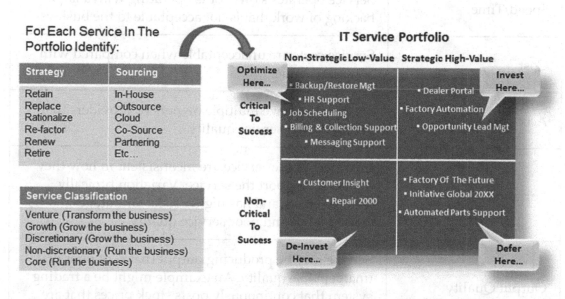

On the right hand side, each service has been placed into a quadrant that distinguishes the value and contribution of that service to the overall business:

   - The upper right quadrant shows services that may be directly bringing in revenue to the business organization. These services may imply a prioritized investment strategy.

- The upper left of the quadrant shows services that are not strategic but must be delivered to keep the business running. These services may imply a cost reduction and optimization strategy.

- Those services in the lower left of the quadrant may represent opportunities for cost reduction since they provide no value or are not needed.

- The bottom right of the quadrant identifies services that may be coming up in the future. These may represent early indicators of funding actions that may need to be considered for the future.

3. Identify what improvements need to be made to services by using the output of the Step 4 assessment findings and recommendations. A technique called Lens Analysis can be applied to identify what improvements may need to be made. This technique looks at each service with different views. These are:

Lens Type	Description
Frustration	Service has low customer satisfaction levels with many complaints.
Labor	Service consumes an inordinate amount of manual labor to produce.
Speed/Time	Service operates slowly or is operating with a large backlog of work that is not acceptable to the business.
Cost	Service costs are unacceptable when compared with service revenue
Accountability	Service may have multiple owners or providers that are hindering service quality.
Variation	Providers of the service are inconsistent in how they deliver or support the service. Variation typically leads to errors and has higher risks for outages, wasted labor and poor service quality.
Output Quality	Service may be producing output that is of poor or unacceptable quality. An example might be a trading system that continuously posts stock prices that are inaccurate.

Each service should be analyzed using the above lenses. The purpose of using the lens approach is to ensure that a broad mindset is taken as improvement actions are reviewed and finalized. It is not unusual to find multiple lens areas that may be uncovered when analyzing each service.

As improvement opportunities are identified, those opportunities should be listed in an inventory. Prioritize the inventory. It is highly likely that more improvement actions may be identified than can be acted upon by the IT organization. Therefore, a scoring approach should be used to prioritize which activities may yield the best benefits. An example of a scoring approach might look like the following:

Area	Scoring Criteria	Points
Benefit	Will provide significant benefits or major risks exist if project not done	9
	Will provide some benefits or moderate risk if project not done	3
	Will provide little or few benefits and little risk exists if the project is not done	1
Cost	Carries low project costs e.g. < $50K	9
	Carries moderate project costs e.g. $50-150K	3
	Carries high project costs e.g. > $150K	1
Effort	Project can be completed in less than 3 months	9
	Project can be completed in 3-6 months	3
	Project may exceed 9 months in duration	1
Risk	Project has few or no risks in the way of success	9
	Project carries moderate levels of risk for success	3
	Project carries high levels of risk for success	1

For each improvement opportunity, determine a score (1, 3 or 9) for each criteria type (benefit, cost, effort and risk). Then sum the four values to get a total project score. Using the business impact score, opportunities can now be ranked by importance and contribution to the business.

4. Now group efforts into strategic projects summarizing the prioritized inventory of service improvements. A high level project charter and description of each project along with its estimated costs should be developed. Summarize the project information into an overall service improvement strategy roadmap. This should be reviewed and approved by the IT executive management.

At this point, a service strategy and improvement plan has been developed that can now be acted upon by the IT organization. Key benefits from applying this strategy are:

- Positioning IT executives to articulate their services, service costs and demand in a manner that provides transparency of IT spend to the business, optimizes costs and improves service quality

- Establishing an IT service strategy that clearly links IT projects and services to the business priorities and contribution areas which they support

- Gaining a jump start on IT service management and other service initiatives in a manner that provides bottom line business benefit.

Strategic Sourcing

Let's look again at the portfolio model presented in Step 5 of the preceding section. This time we'll look at the left hand side of the diagram:

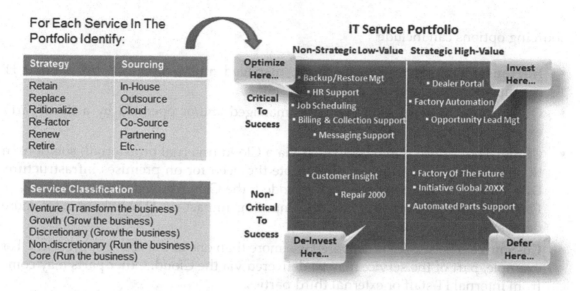

In developing the Service Strategy, several key build and delivery decisions need to be made for each service:

Strategy

Should we retain the service? Fix it? Remove it? Should we just keep it running? Identify the overall direction for what should happen with the service over the next 1-2 years.

Sourcing

Who delivers the service? Is this done by internal IT staff or an outsourcing provider? If sourced from more than one provider, what pieces and parts will each provider be responsible for?

Let's answer the Strategy question first. Strategy options can include:

- **Retain**. In this case, the service is kept as is. Investments remain flat or minimally changed.

- **Replace**. In this case, the service will be kept, but the underlying solution that delivers that service will be replaced. This will involve a specific project to be tied to the service and the service will incur one-time build costs for the replacement.

- **Rationalize**. In this case, the service will be kept, but underlying solutions that deliver that service may be combined or consolidated with other service solutions.

- **Re-Factor**. In this case, the service will be kept, but investments will be made in improving the service to make it more efficient or wean out deficiencies and problems that may exist with it.

- **Renew**. In this case, the service in question may have been previously retired, but there is a desire to re-start it up again.
- **Retire**. In this case, a decision has been made tio retire and decommission the service.

Sourcing options can include:

- **In-House**. The service will be built, managed and/or operated by internal IT organization development and support staff.
- **Outsource**. The service will be built, managed and/or operated by a third party external supplier.
- **Cloud**. The service will be delivered via a Cloud (internal or external) solution. In this case, the Cloud provider will negate the need for on premises infrastructure. Depending on the level of service provided, the Cloud provider may deliver IaaS, PaaS or AaaS support (see Cloud Computing Impact on ITSM chapter for more details).
- **Co-Source**. The service is delivered use more than one of the above approaches. For example, part of the service may be delivered via the Cloud. Other parts may come from internal IT staff or external third parties.
- **Partnering**. The service is Co-Sourced, but each party in the Co-Sourcing agreement will have equal status in how the service is managed and delivered. Examples of these might include a consortium of research companies that fund and provide focused research information and support for a specific industry area or support need.

Chapter 13

Driving Out Waste With CSI

Becoming A Lean Service Provider

Developing an overall journey towards becoming a lean service provider doesn't happen overnight. This requires a changes in technology, development and operating processes and organizational roles and responsibilities. It requires a long term vision and commitment by senior executive leadership to be successful. It does not happen simply by buying new tools or adopting the latest frameworks and methodologies.

Here is a suggested model for undertaking the transformation to a High Velocity ITSM Service Provider:

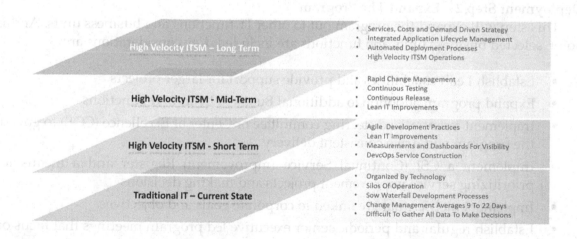

Consider the journey to levels 2, 3 and 4 in the above diagram in 3 key phases (it is assumed you are starting out from Level 1). These are described below:

Deployment Step 1 – Getting Started

This step is the starting point. Here you will begin the journey to establish a Lean culture within the IT organization. This includes identifying key staff resources to be involved and seeking out 1-2 business issues or problems that can serve as early wins.

The main goal of this step is to develop proof of concept and demonstrate value. Key considerations are:

- Stay focused in a single Business Unit or Function
- Address a specific business issue or pain point
- Develop action plans and training to imbed lean, agile and DevOps concepts into the IT organization
- Develop limited and basic Lean capabilities in terms of processes, tools and organizational roles and responsibilities
- Develop a foundation of core Lean capabilities to support the execution of Lean projects; Lean capabilities include:
  - Training and certification
  - Program Governance
  - Methodology and tools
  - Prioritization of Lean initiatives
- Establish a consistent continual service improvement methodology that will be used
- Provide coaching and learning opportunities for IT staff and to support personal development plans
- Focus on individual processes
- Link efforts to Business Unit / Function goals and objectives
- Test and validate Lean practices through the execution of at least two pilot initiatives
- Identify delivered value to validate the effectiveness of Lean initiatives

Deployment Step 2 – Expand The Program

This step will expand the program out to other IT functions and business units. At this point, selected business units and functions are included. Key considerations are:

- Establish Lean capabilities and provide support for larger projects
- Expand program adoption to additional Business Units and Functions
- Implement a centralized steering committee or Center of Excellence (COE) to govern the program and drive consistent delivery
- Implement a CSI (Continual Service Improvement) Register and a means for prioritizing service improvement projects and making decisions
- Implement metrics that are linked to corporate goals and objectives
- Establish regular and periodic senior executive led program meetings that focus on prioritizing and funding lean projects

Deployment Step 3 – Imbed Into The Enterprise

This step will cement the program to the IT and business enterprise. At this point, all business units and functions are included. Key considerations are:

- Deploy lean practices to the entire enterprise
- Obtain sponsorship from CXO level executives

- Focus on end-to-end services
- Integrate and formalize Lean organization change and communications
- Implement an enterprise lean infrastructure of processes, tools and organization responsibilities

Strategy On A Page: The Lean CSI Program

Development of a Lean CSI (Continual Service Improvement) Program is key towards governing and managing the many Lean initiatives, projects and priorities that will be taking place. High velocity ITSM does not have a finite end to Lean activities. They continue ongoing and are part of the High Velocity ITSM eco-sphere.

Strategy on a page presents the overall program on a single presentation slide. Here it is shown below:

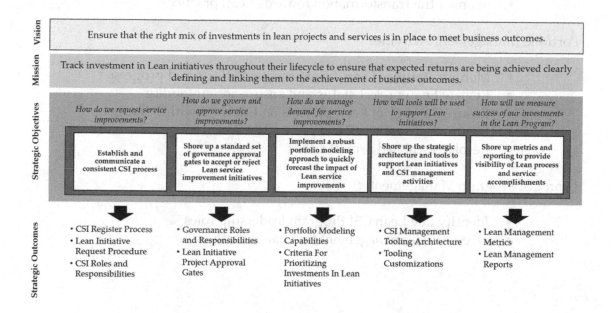

With this, a concise overview of the program is shown that can be shared with executives and IT staff who are seeking to understand what the program is all about. Within the diagram, the mission, objectives and key initiatives are all presented on a single page. For each key initiative, key outcomes are listed. These show what would be developed as part of the program.

Details on an actual process for running the program are described in the next section of this chapter.

Lean CSI Program Roles and Responsibilities

In addition to roles for implementing Lean projects and changes, 3 Key roles will be needed to run and operate the Lean CSI Program. These roles are used to govern and manage the CSI Register which is essentially a portfolio of Lean CSI projects. Listed below are the roles with their key activities:

Investment Board

This role has the highest authority for the Lean CSI Program. It sponsors the program and manages the investment streams and funding for Lean CSI projects and initiatives.

Portfolio Planning Activities

- Affirm strategic priorities and outcomes
- Prioritize IT investments across competing interests
- Initiate new Lean projects aligned with strategy
- Identify project leads for new projects
- Balance trade-offs in business process change versus IT customization
- Sponsor the transformation towards Lean practices

Portfolio Management Activities

- Monitor status of Lean Transformation efforts and progress
- Review Lean project status and ensure accountability
- Ensure delivery of Lean projects on time and within budget
- Ensure realization of Lean project benefits
- Resolve escalated project issues

Lean CSI Program Management

- Identify key Lean CSI Program leadership roles
- Oversee risk management for Lean initiatives

Portfolio Manager

This role manages the Lean CSI Portfolio (CSI Register). It works with the business, IT planning and Finance to assemble the Portfolio and monitors the Portfolio as initiatives change.

Portfolio Planning Activities

- Work with Business, IT planning and Finance to establish priorities and identify constraints
- Maintain long-term (2 year time horizon) plans for the CSI Register

Portfolio Management Activities

- Work with project Sponsors, business functions and IT to coordinate execution of current Lean initiatives
- Measures the realization of benefits
- Reviews status of Lean initiatives and updates the Portfolio as needed

Lean CSI Program Management

- Manages continuous improvement of the Lean CSI Program and Portfolio management process
- Facilitates the delivery of timely, accurate information on Lean initiative status and value

Business Unit Leadership

This role manages the Lean CSI Portfolio (CSI Register). It works with the business, IT planning and Finance to assemble the Portfolio and monitors the Portfolio as initiatives change.

Portfolio Planning Activities

- Maintains alignment with and provides input on:
  - Strategic priorities
  - Release management plans
  - Customer contact blueprint
  - System development roadmap
  - Long term capital plan (in cases of multi-year projects)

Portfolio Management Activities

- Provides management of:
  - Lean project objectives and outcomes
  - New or unmet business requirements
  - New proposed Lean projects

Lean CSI Program Management

- Provides project-level status to the Investment Board including:
  - Schedule and timing of Lean initiatives
  - Planned and actual costs for approved Lean projects
  - Risk management of Lean projects
  - Benefit realization from Lean projects

Lean CSI Program Activities

This section describes the key steps and activities for running a Lean CSI Program. If you came here to understand specific steps for how to improve a process or service, that is presented as one of the tools in the ITSM Lean Toolkit in the next chapter (Improvement Process Roadmap Tool).

A recommended approach is to establish a Lean CSI Program. Identified lean improvement activities in the program will be grouped into Lean initiatives. These are implemented as project efforts. Each Lean initiative will be recorded in the CSI Register which is essentially a portfolio of investments in CSI (or in this case Lean) activities.

A high level view of the Lean CSI Program is presented below:

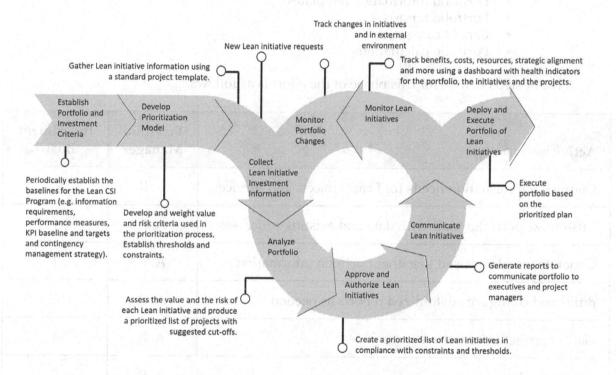

A set of activities for each step in the Program is described on the following pages. Along with each activity, roles and responsibilities have been mapped to each activity shown using the RACI (R=Responsible, A=Accountable, C=Consulted and I=Informed) nomenclature.

Establish Portfolio and Investment Criteria

This phase sets up the Portfolio (CSI Register) and investment criteria.

Key inputs of this activity are:

- Project and service proposals
- Existing project and service management processes
- Business constraints and thresholds
- Business Strategic Plans
- Financial constraints and thresholds

Key outputs from this activity will include:

- Portfolio information templates
- Portfolio reports
- Benefit categories
- Portfolio calculations

A list of steps to take for this phase of the effort is as follows:

Activities	Portfolio Manager	Investment Board
Define the information needs for Lean projects and services	A, R	C
Customize portfolio tools with data and existing processes	A, R	I
Generate templates used to gather portfolio information	A, R	I
Build and configure customized reports as needed	A, R	C
Gather project information	A, R	I
Categorize benefits	A, R	C
Determine the desired portfolio composition based on types of investments (e.g. Innovation, productivity, growth and maintenance)	A, R	C
Choose and weight prioritization criteria for each investment type	R	A
Define criteria, weightings and calculations for Strategic Value and Complexity scores	R	A
Input annual business constraints and other thresholds	A, R	C

Develop The Prioritization Model

This phase sets up the business rules by which investments in Lean initiatives will be prioritized.

Key inputs of this activity are:

- Prioritization Criteria
- Lessons Learned
- Existing Portfolio
- Investment Status
- Project and Service Performance
- Strategy and Directions
- Market, Industry and Technical Trends

Key outputs from this activity will include:

- Prioritization Criteria
- Qualification or Screenings
- Evaluation and Prioritizations
- CSI Register Process Flow and Documentation

A list of steps to take for this phase of the effort is as follows:

Activities	Portfolio Manager	Investment Board
Develop, review, approve and maintain decision criteria (Decision Criteria consist of: Qualification or Screening, and Evaluation or Prioritization	R	A
Develop and maintain the investment portfolio status process	A, R	
Update investment portfolio	A, R	
Request update to strategic and tactical plans, as required	R	A

Collect Lean Initiative Investment Information

This phase pulls together all the information on Lean initiatives so they can be later analyzed.

Key inputs of this activity are:

- Lean Initiative Investment Proposal
- Business Case Recommendation
- Resource Availability
- Affordability with current budgets and allocations

Key outputs from this activity will include:

- Lean Initiative Investment Decision
- Business Case Recommendation

A list of steps to take for this phase of the effort is as follows:

Activities	Portfolio Manager	Investment Board
Evaluate Investment Proposal against Investment Screening Criteria	C	A,R
Review investment proposal	C	A, R
Decide if Investment Proposal qualifies for possible inclusion in the portfolio	I	A,R
Review Business Case recommendation	C	
Validate Business Case with current environment	C	
Obtain Business Case Authorization as required	C	
Finalize Business Case summary and recommendation/ rejection	I	

Analyze Portfolio

This phase reviews all the information on Lean initiatives and analyzes them to determine which ones will receive funding and go forward.

Key inputs of this activity are:

- Business Case Authorized Recommendation
- Resource Availability
- Approved Portfolio

Key outputs from this activity will include:

- Portfolio Recommendations
- Investment Status and Performance

A list of steps to take for this phase of the effort is as follows:

Activities	Portfolio Manager	Investment Board
Assign portfolio ranking	A. R	C
Normalize portfolio ranking	A, R	C
Revalidate affordability	A, R	I
Review portfolio status and performance	R	A
Identify strategy and portfolio options and scenarios	R	A, R
Model options and scenarios	A, R	C
Update/Modify portfolio recommendations	R	A
Align the portfolio with key value drivers	A, R	C
Model impact of new Lean initiatives, services and changes on the existing portfolio	A, R	I
Define the risks and values for each Lean initiative in order to prioritize them	A, R	C
Prioritize Lean initiatives and services	A, R	C

Approve and Authorize Lean Initiatives

This phase reviews all the information on Lean initiatives and analyzes them to determine which ones will receive funding and go forward.

Key inputs of this activity are:

- Portfolio Recommendations
- Resource Availability
- Fit With Current Budgets and Strategies

Key outputs from this activity will include:

- Portfolio Updates
- Approvals to Proceed
- Authorized Funding

A list of steps to take for this phase of the effort is as follows:

Activities	Investment Board
Review and confirm Portfolio ranking of investments.	A, R
Provide direction on each investment to proceed (e.g. cancel, suspend or continue)	A, R
Provide funding for investments	A, R

Communicate Lean Initiatives

This phase communicates Lean initiatives and their funding status to business and IT stakeholders and Project Managers.

Key inputs of this activity are:

- Portfolio dashboard(s)
- Performance and Status information
- Current portfolio costs and revenues
- Planned benefits and actuals realized to date

Key outputs from this activity will include:

- Updated portfolio dashboard(s)
- Summary of Lean initiative costs and benefits
- Recommendations to current plans and strategies based on current portfolio performance and results

A list of steps to take for this phase of the effort is as follows:

Activities	Portfolio Manager	Investment Board
Upload portfolio status and performance information	A, R	I
Follow the Portfolio Management Dashboard	A, R	I
Provide recommendations to plans and strategies as needed	A, R	C
Report by project, sponsor, investment type, milestone, etc.	A, R	I
Prepare summary of portfolio cost and benefits	A, R	I
Generate and communicate the portfolio alignment map, for a specific year or for the next planning period (e.g. 5 years)	A, R	I
Establish the next years financial plan to be integrated in the strategic planning cycle	R	A

Monitor Lean Initiatives

This phase monitors progress of Lean initiatives and updates portfolio information and status to business and IT stakeholders and Project Managers.

Key inputs of this activity are:

- Portfolio dashboard(s)
- Performance and Status information
- Current portfolio costs and revenues
- Planned benefits and actuals realized to date

Key outputs from this activity will include:

- Updated portfolio dashboard(s)
- Summary of Lean initiative costs and benefits
- Recommendations to current plans and strategies based on current portfolio performance and results

A list of steps to take for this phase of the effort is as follows:

Activities	Portfolio Manager	Investment Board
Upload portfolio status and performance information	A, R	I
Compared expected and realized benefit tracking	A, R	I
Monitor impact of new business constraints (new regulation, increase in competition, budget reduction, downsizing, etc.) on planned investment	A, R	C
Track benefits in accordance with strategic plans	A, R	C
Provide recommendations to plans and strategies as needed	A, R	C
Report by project, project, sponsor, investment type, milestone date, etc.	A, R	I
Prepare summary of portfolio cost and benefits	A, R	I

Monitor Portfolio Changes

This phase monitors the Portfolio of Lean initiatives for business or technology changes and updates the portfolio with those changes.

Key inputs of this activity are:

- Business unit needs and issues
- Management criteria and guidance

Key outputs from this activity will include:

- Project and service charter
- Cost and benefits estimates

A list of steps to take for this phase of the effort is as follows:

Activities	Project or Service Requestor	Portfolio Manager (PMO)
Identify resources and requirements changes for Lean initiatives and project changes	A, R	
Encapsulate business needs into Lean initiatives and services	A, R	
Develop Lean initiative and service charters	A, R	C
Identify Lean initiative business cases and cost estimates	A, R	C
Submit proposals for management approvals	A, R	R

Deploy and Execute Portfolio Of Lean Initiatives

This phase launches each approved Lean initiative and updates the portfolio as those efforts proceed.

Key inputs of this activity are:

- Project Status Reports
- Project Work Plans
- Project Financial Reports
- Issues/Action Item Logs
- Project Schedules

Key outputs from this activity will include:

- Project Performance Summaries
- Project And Service Costs – Planned Versus Actuals
- Summary Of Project Or Service Issue
- Portfolio Updates

A list of steps to take for this phase of the effort is as follows:

Activities	IT and Business Units	Business Relationship Managers	IT Leadership
Gather current project and service status and information	A, R	R	R
Review project and service progress and attainment	A, R	R	R
Identify key project and service issues	A, R	R	R
Identify project/service mitigation actions and recommendations where needed	A, R	R	R
Provide portfolio updates	A, R	R	R
Provide status and performance reports	A, R	R	R

Example Of A CSI Lean Project Governance Cycle

It is common for most IT organizations to execute on a cycle of planning at the executive level for investments in projects and initiatives. Presented here is a set of activities gathered from several IT organizations for governing their project investments. Planning for which Lean initiatives to invest in follows this kind of cycle.

First Quarter Governance Activities (e.g. Jan-Mar)

- Release of the new CSI Register (portfolio of Lean initiatives)
- Launch new Lean initiatives
- CSI Register check and Portfolio validation
- Current and previous year portfolio updates
- Strategic and tactical input from business leadership

Second Quarter Governance Activities (e.g. Apr-Jun)

- Review and readjust capital and operating allocations for the current year
- Brainstorm Lean initiatives for next year
- Review current Lean initiatives and pending proposals current status against desired outcomes
- Update current and previous year Lean initiatives
- Implement CSI Register/Portfolio changes (based on current business strategy, technologies, etc.)
- Conduct strategic look ahead for the CSI Register/Portfolio

Third Quarter Governance Activities (e.g. Jul-Sep)

- Plan and prioritize next year's Lean initiatives
- Revise long term capital and operating plans
- Confirm project sponsors for Lean initiatives
- Define Lean project outcomes
- Start pitching plans to IT and business unit leadership
- Review current CSI Register/Portfolio and pending proposals current status against desired outcomes

Fourth Quarter Governance Activities (e.g. Oct-Dec)

- Finalize portfolio of Lean initiatives for next year
- Receive budget approval for Lean initiatives
- Allocate capital to Lean initiative projects
- Review current CSI Register/Portfolio and pending proposals current status against desired outcomes

Breaking Out Of Firefighting Mode

Some IT organizations find that they have no time to pursue service improvements. "Too much is going on" they will say. "It is one thing after another", or, "We have so many incidents to deal with there is no time to fix anything". This chapter addresses IT organizations that may be in such a bind.

It firefighting results in high amounts of unplanned labor which puts major constraints on growth and innovation objectives. It indicates low velocity in delivery of IT services. Fixing incidents and problems in itself is non-value. Worse yet, it is unplanned when it happens. This means IT has to take away valuable time from productive work and address tasks that were never planned for. It is costly and it slows everything down that IT is trying to do.

The bottom line is that firefighting is not just an IT problem – it is a major business issue that drains significant costs and constrains the business from achieving its strategic objectives. Since most of firefighting is unplanned labor, it is easy to build a business case for addressing it.

Imagine coming into an executive's office showing your IT costs with the following scenario:

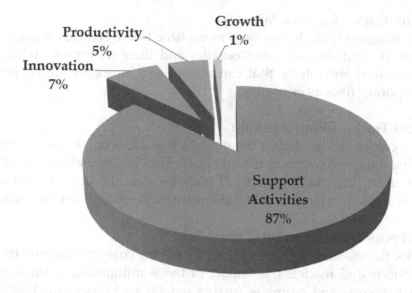

If the IT labor budget is $50M then this means $43.5M is being wasted on non-value unplanned activities. Not a good story that anyone wants to see. Yet many IT organizations are exactly in this bind. How to get out of it?

The suggested strategy is to implement a tactical approach to quickly contain the situation and then strategically move forward. This approach is pictured as follows:

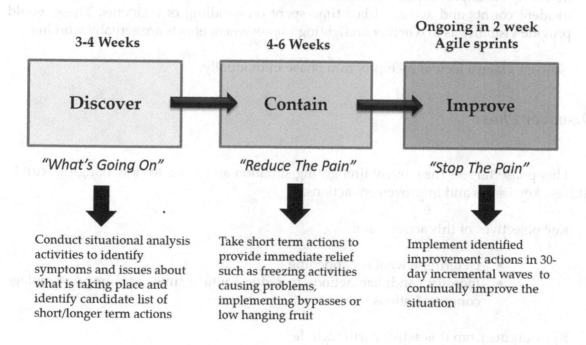

This approach will operated as a program. 4 parallel tracks of effort will take place simultaneously. Each track represents a focus area described as follows:

Incident Focus Track – Reduces Pain
Identifies low hanging fruit that reduces mean-time-to-fix, reduces impacts of outages, and increases communications about outages and their resolution status. This track focuses on the short term items that can make life a bit easier for IT: workarounds, bypasses, temporary fixes as examples.

Problem Focus Track – Eliminates Pain
Identifies root causes that underpin the outages that are occurring and removes errors that are causing outages to occur in the first place. This is essentially a proactive Problem Management effort. It is the most critical track because the outcomes of track efforts actually reduce overall incident counts and ensure incidents will not recur again.

Availability Focus Track – Prevents Future Pain
Identifies risks, threats and likelihoods that exist in the current infrastructure, develops mitigation actions and models the impact of those mitigations if implemented. The modeling part projects and estimates further reductions in incidents that might occur if mitigations were put into place. This is to help identify business cases for future improvement investments.

Visibility Focus Track – See The Pain
Identifies a core set of KPIs, CSFs and operational metrics that indicate the health of the infrastructure from an availability point of view and allow for informed management decisions on improvement actions to take. A key set of metrics would include overall incident counts and average labor time spent on handling of incidents. These would provide visibility as to whether firefighting improvement efforts are actually working.

Now let's take a look at each program phase individually:

Discover Phase

This phase targets the current firefighting situation and looks for low hanging fruit to address key issues and improvement actions.

Key objectives of this activity are:

- Determine what is happening
- Identify candidate actions to reduce outage times and improve outage communications

Key outputs from this activity will include:

- Prioritized backlog of mitigation actions to undertake
- Current state risk model

- Health status report

A list of steps to take for this phase of the effort is as follows:

Focus Area	Steps To Take
Incident Focus	• Interview key stakeholders • Inventory candidate actions • Prioritize actions • Identify key technology issues • Identify actions to reduce outage times • Identify key process issues • Identify actions to bypass or reduce outage times • Identify skills and communication issues • Identify actions to mitigate issues • Identify supplier issues • Identify actions to mitigate issues
Problem Focus	• Review incident logs for trends • Identify candidate list of actions • Prioritize actions • Identify root causes • Identify known errors
Availability Focus	• Identify risks • Identify likelihoods • Identify potential mitigation actions • Prioritize mitigation actions
Visibility Focus	• Identify what needs to be measured • Identify current measurement capabilities • Create short term list of measurements • Identify responsibilities for Health Status reporting • Identified unplanned labor levels • Identify supplier performance metrics and issues

Contain Phase

This phase implements short term fixes and low hanging fruit to ease the pain and fence off firefighting conditions.

Key objectives of this activity are:

- Implement short term actions and bypasses
- Measure and report on results and progress
- Finalize improvement roadmap

Key outputs from this activity will include:

- Prioritized backlog of mitigation actions
- Current state risk model (Risks, Occurrences, Mitigations)
- Health status report

A list of steps to take for this phase of the effort is as follows:

Focus Area	Steps To Take
Incident Focus	- Coordinate implementation actions to put in bypasses and short term fixes - Confirm results
Problem Focus	- Coordinate implementation actions to remove root causes of incidents - Confirm results
Availability Focus	- Build and confirm roadmap for future service improvement actions - Implement short-term actions - Model impact of proposed future actions
Visibility Focus	- Report on progress

Improve Phase

This phase will use agile efforts to continually execute actions every 2 weeks to draw down the amount of labor spent on firefighting.

Key objectives of this activity are:

- Implement longer term improvement actions that can be completed within 2 week sprints
- Measure and report on results and progress
- Identify sprint iterations that will take place and what improvements will be addressed

Key outputs from this activity will include:

- Health Status Reports (weekly)
- Risk impact results for future actions
- Actions to be taken for each (next) sprint iteration

A list of steps to take for this phase of the effort is as follows. Note that these activities are ongoing for as long as necessary. They will occur in 2-week sprints:

Focus Area	Steps To Take
Incident Focus	• Coordinate implementation actions for reducing impact of incidents • Identify backlog for next sprint iteration • Implement improvement actions for each sprint • Review results
Problem Focus	• Coordinate implementation actions for eliminating root causes • Identify backlog for next sprint iteration • Implement improvement actions for each sprint • Review results
Availability Focus	• Review improvement progress • Identify backlog for next sprint iteration • Implement longer-term actions (actions that can be taken every 2 weeks) • Model impact of proposed future actions • Review results
Visibility Focus	• Report on progress

To execute on all this, a SWAT team approach is suggested to execute on the program, gain momentum and break out of firefighting mode. It is suggested that an overall Team Leader be provided to lead the effort. This can come out of the management ranks or the Problem Management function. A single point of contact authority should be in place for each of the 4 focus areas described earlier. Overall, the Program Organizational Model might look like the following:

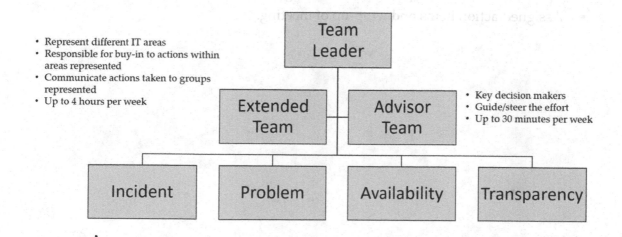

- Represent different IT areas
- Responsible for buy-in to actions within areas represented
- Communicate actions taken to groups represented
- Up to 4 hours per week

- Key decision makers
- Guide/steer the effort
- Up to 30 minutes per week

Key success factors for this effort and program team are as follows:

- The Core Team must be at least 50% dedicated
- Advisor team has authority to make decisions and demonstrate commitment to the program
- The program has executive sponsorship and buy-in
- Improvement actions have buy-in from affected IT and business units (Extended Team consists of business stakeholders who have responsibility for this)
- Improvement actions should be implemented using less than 15% additional effort over and above current staff responsibilities

Conducting A Service Review Meeting

Service Review meetings provide a very important role in reviewing service quality, attainment of service performance goals and gauging business satisfaction with the service. The meeting enables Continual Service Improvement activities to take place and be formally tracked. This section provides a suggested agenda for a Service Review meeting. The list of items on the agenda is not exhaustive but is meant to provide at least some minimal guidance for these kinds of meetings might be conducted.

The suggested agenda is as follows:

- Review minutes and actions (and their status) from the previous Service Review Meeting
- Summary of current service attainment and any key service issues for the period
- Business Relationship Manager report(s) on business unit satisfaction and key issues for the period since the last review
- Status on current service improvement programs
- Planned service changes for the coming period
- Update of the CSI (Continual Service Improvement) Register
- Agreed actions to take place for addressing service issues
- Assigned action items and wrap-up of meeting.

Chapter

14

ITSM Lean Toolkit

Overview

The following pages present different kinds of tools and techniques that you might employ to find waste, lean out processes, brainstorm improvement ideas and resolve issues. Each tool is briefly described along with simple steps for using it and the kind of situations where it may best be used.

A summary of the tools described is listed below along with a general guide as to where they might be used. Tool descriptions are presented in alphabetical order so you can quickly find them.

The following groups the tools by general categories of where they might be used. Further information is provided with each tool description.

Finding and removing waste:
- Cell Design
- Eight Deadly Wastes
- Non-Value Step Analysis
- Process Lead Time Analysis
- Value Stream Map

Setting strategy and a course of action:
- Advantages/Disadvantages Table
- Affinity Map
- Brainstorm
- Crawford Slip List
- Nominal Group Technique
- Prioritization Matrix
- SWOT Analysis

Determining the causes of issues and identifying appropriate action plans to address them:

- Cause and Effect Diagram
- Box Plot
- Check Sheet
- Correlation Analysis
- Data Collection Plan
- Data Selection Sample
- Design Of Experiments (DOE)
- Fault Tree Analysis
- Five Whys
- Histogram
- Observation Post
- Pain Value Analysis
- Pareto Analysis
- Storyboard

Effecting organizational change and dealing with people and stakeholders:

- Organizational Change Flow Of Activities
- Organizational Change Success Factors
- Principled Negotiation Method
- Stakeholder Map

Understanding current state processes and issues:

- Process Mapping
- Regression Analysis
- SIPOC Diagram

Dealing with operating risks:

- Failure Mode and Effects Analysis (FMEA)
- Risk Mitigation Matrix

Understanding customer needs and requirements:

- Critical-To-Quality (CTQ) Tree
- Kano Analysis

Developing, managing and tracking improvement efforts:

- Business Case
- Continual Service Improvement (CSI) Register
- Improvement Process Roadmap
- Issue Log
- Kaizen Program
- Kanban Board

Advantages/Disadvantages Table

Description:

This tool can be used to deal with intermittent issues that appear to happen randomly or appear to come and go and cannot be recreated or repeated. It can also be used to identify an improvement decision where it is unclear which course to take. Works best in a group setting where lots of ideas can be generated.

Best Use:

Deciding whether to pursue an improvement opportunity when the direction to do so is not clear. It is also helpful when multiple solutions are in play and a decision needs to be made to select only one.

How To Use:

1. Lay out the table as shown below
2. Brainstorm the pros and cons in the table
3. If there is more than one alternative, use a separate table for each
4. Discuss the pros and cons listed in the table
5. Provide each team member with 10 votes
6. Team members place as many of their allotted votes on one or more of the pros or cons
7. Sum the votes in either column
8. Consider pursuing the improvement opportunity if the advantages column scores higher than the disadvantages column
9. Choose the best if there is more than one alternative.

Example:

Improve Cloud Identity and Security	
Advantages	**Disadvantages**
Closes many security vulnerabilities in the current platform	Product licensing is expensive (more than $500K)
Reduces number of domain sign-ins that users need to make to get to their applications	Disruptive to current technology skills available in-house and familiar way of operating
Provides access control by user, device type, application and many other means versus just IP address	Delays implementation of other Cloud initiatives by 4-5 months
Fully supported by many leading vendors	Will require additional integration with on-premises server-based applications
Supports the corporate mobility strategy to access applications from any device	

Affinity Map

Description:
This tool can be used to organize large amounts of data (ideas, opinions, issues) into groupings based on common characteristics.

Best Use:
Best used in conjunction with any brainstorming exercise to determine what solutions should be applied to an issue.

How To Use:
1. Key concepts, such as potential solutions, are written on individual cards and adhered to a wall or white board
2. Participants and/or the facilitator should then move the cards so that they are grouped by similar traits
3. A "header" should then be developed for each group for future identification

The wall or white board may look like the following example:

Resistance To New Ways Of Working	Lack Of Planning	Organizational Issues And Challenges	Challenging Management Culture	Poor Data For Decision Making
Lack Of Compelling Vision	Plan Products Without Process	Lack Of Management Commitment	Competition Versus Cooperation	Poor Data Collection Process
Stakeholder Resistance To Change	Poor Requirements Planning	Little Funding For Training	Pressure For Success	Lack Of Technology To Collect Data
No Incentives To Change	Start Activities Without Any Planning	People Too Busy To Learn New Skills	Few Incentives For Good Ideas	Current Data Is Inaccurate
People Don't Work Well Together	Poor Resource Commitments To Plans		Reactive Versus Proactive	Few Reports And Dashboards
Lack Of Trust In New Methods			Lack Of Management Understanding	Lack Of Trust In Data Collected

Box Plot

Description:
This tool can be used to present a quick graphical representation of five key observations of a set of data. The box plot displays the minimum, maximum, first quartile, median, and third quartile measurements of a data set. It also displays outliers individually.

Best Use:
Quickly displaying numeric results from a complex set of data on a single slide or page to get the big picture of what the data is showing.

How To Use:

1. Calculate the five key observation values: minimum, 1st quartile, median, 3rd quartile, and maximum
2. Plot all five points vertically aligned with the parameter value on the vertical axis
3. Draw a box around the quartile markings to encompass the mean
4. Connect the minimum and maximum values with the box as shown below:

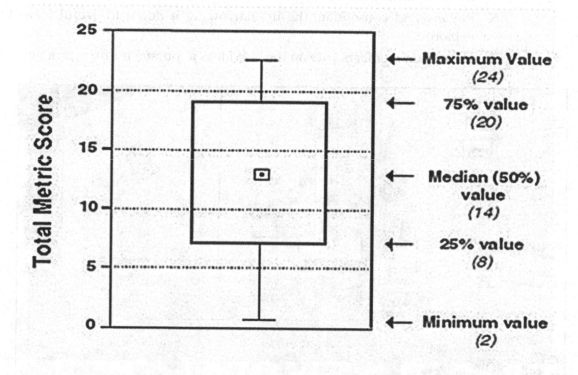

Brainstorm

Description:
This tool can be used to spark creativity within a large group and capitalize on the useful contribution of all team members. The goal is to quickly develop a high volume list of ideas on a specific topic that is developed free from criticism and judgment.

Best Use:
Quickly gathering all team member ideas and contributions with a structured approach and determining a course of action.

How To Use:
1. Assemble the team or group
2. Define the specific objective or goal of the exercise
3. Give team members some amount of time to individually identify their ideas (typically 10-15 minutes)
4. Have each team member present their ideas, in round robin fashion, one at a time
5. Record each idea on flip chart, making sure it is understood and making no criticism or judgment
6. Review and consolidate the list narrowing it down to useful ideas to explore
7. Have team members vote on the best ideas to pursue for further action

Business Case

Description:

This tool can be used to justify the resources, investment, and changes that are necessary to initiate an improvement project.

Best Use:

Situations where management buy-in and agreement need to be obtained in order to fund an improvement effort.

How To Use:

1. Identify the possible improvement options
2. Gather data (financial, performance, quality, and so on) on feasibility and specifics of each option
3. Focus and refine the options, incorporating the data
4. Align options to the corporate or IT business mission
5. Identify one-time (project) and ongoing (maintenance) costs for each option
6. Calculate the cash outlay over a selected time period (e.g. 24 months) for each option
7. Calculate the return-on-investment (ROI) over the selected time period for each option
8. Outline and justify each option

Business Case Presentation Outline

A. Purpose Of Solution Being Proposed
   - Justification for the solution
   - Benefits to be gained (e.g. cost savings, time, speed, quality, risk mitigation
B. Success Criteria (e.g. measurements and outcomes that show success)
C. Solution Approach Options (try to show no more than 3)
   1. Option 1 Approach
      - High level approach plan
      - Pros (e.g. Benefits achieved or lower cost alternative)
      - Cons (e.g. Benefits not achieved or risks involved)
      - Return on investment (ROI)
      - High level schedule for when benefits will be realized
      - Key risks and mitigation actions
   2. Option 2 Approach (...same as above for Option 1...)
   3. Option 3 Approach (...same as above for Option 1...)
D. Recommended Solution Approach (which Option is recommended)
E. Next Steps To Be Taken (e.g. to finalize decision and funding)

Cause and Effect Diagram

Description:
This tool is commonly called the Cause and Effect diagram, Fishbone or Ishikawa diagram (after its creator Dr. Kaoru Ishikawa). It can be used to help identify all the possible or probable sources of a given problem or issue. Once developed, this list of potential causes can be narrowed down to root causes using other methods such as Pareto Analysis (described later in this chapter).

Best Use:
Identifying the underlying possible causes of problems and issues.

How To Use:
1. Define the problem to be solved and record on the left side of the diagram
2. List categories showing each on a separate thread or bone
3. Brainstorm potential causes, listing them under the appropriate category
4. Add additional branches or bones to capture causes related to one another
5. Review the resulting list to identify others not yet captured
6. Refine this list using other tools such as Pareto Analysis

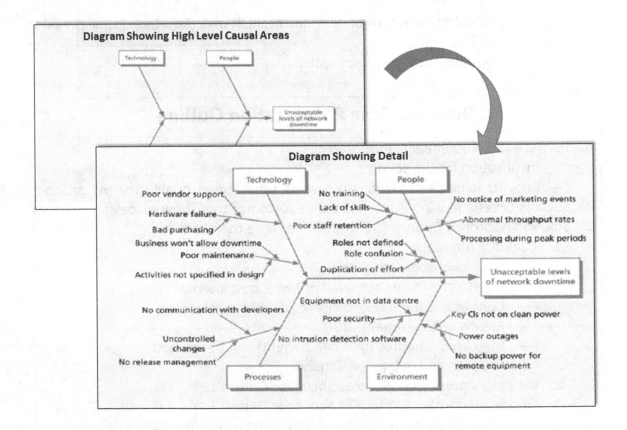

Cell Design

Description:

This tool is used to develop optimal layouts workflows to improve IT ability to maximize throughput, efficiency, and quality. It can improve a process through analysis of the physical layout, movement of data and the process steps and sequence. Many times, workflows are creating inefficiencies such as manually filling out forms and re-entering the same data into a system. Other inefficiencies may exist such as re-keying data from one system to another or needlessly moving data (either physically or electronically) across multiple systems.

Best Use:

Identifying inefficiencies through movement of forms, people and data throughout a workflow.

How To Use:

1. Identify the workflow to be analyzed
2. List each process step of the workflow in sequence
3. Add in data flows around each process step
4. Circle data and workflows to represent each system they are used in
5. Analyze for redundancy and value:
   a. Process steps that add little or no value
   b. Data moving across systems with little or no change
   c. Data being copied from one format to another
6. Identify opportunities to increase flow and efficiency

Example shown below for a password reset workflow without self-service:

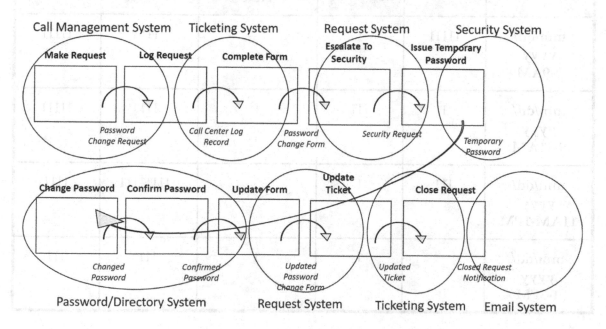

Check Sheet

Description:
This tool provides a structured way to collect data and information on system problems or issues and how often they occur. The focus is on collecting data for specific occurrence of types or locations of defects. They can also be used to record complaint data, server problems etc.

Best Use:
Collecting data to create facts on actual symptoms and issues that can then be used to determine an underlying problem or improvement opportunity.

How To Use:
1. Determine the symptoms, issues and/or types of data that will be collected
2. Develop the check sheet as shown below
3. Take actions to implement the data collection
4. Review data
5. Adjust check sheet if necessary

An example of a check sheet is as follows:

Observance Date and Time	Defect 1 Missing Data	Defect 2 Service Outage	Defect 3 Slow Response Time	Defect 4 Inaccurate Data	Defect 5 Lost User Session
mm/dd/ yyyy 7-9AM	11111	1		111	11111
mm/dd/ yyyy 9-11AM	1	111	1	111	11111
mm/dd/ yyyy 11AM-1PM	111	1		111111111	1111
mm/dd/ yyyy 1-3PM		1	1	111	111

Continual Service Improvement (CSI) Register

Description:
This tool provides a standard means for recording improvement efforts, selecting ones to fund and work on, and then linking these efforts to the IT service portfolio.

Best Use:
Providing transparency for what improvement initiatives have been identified, approved, their status and progress.

How To Use:
1. Establish an ITSM CSI Register and process
2. Define a Continual Service Improvement Process
3. Define CSI Roles and Responsibilities
4. Populate the CSI register with Inventory of CSI requests / initiatives
5. Establish a process for selecting and approving improvement projects
6. Establish CSI Project Approval Gates and criteria
7. Establish Criteria For Prioritizing Investments In CSI Projects
8. Implement tracking and reporting for improvement efforts
9. Link each CSI Register entry with the service(s) it is associated with
10. Update the register on a regular basis as initiatives complete, change or new ones added.

Much more detail on building a CSI Register can be found in the Implementing ITSM book (ISBN: 978-1-4907-1958-0).

The following lists examples of fields that might be tracked in a CSI Register Record
- Opportunity number
- Name or Short Description
- Description
- Date raised
- Current Status
- Effort (Major, Moderate, Minor)
- Link to Project Plan
- Link to Business Case
- Target Completion Date
- Success Criteria and Planned Outcomes
- Effort Estimate
- Cost Estimate
- Priority Score (based on benefits, costs, risks, alignment with strategies)
- Owner
- Raised By
- To be actioned by

Correlation Analysis

Description:

This tool provides a technique for investigating the strength of the relationship between two quantitative, continuous variables. The strength of correlation is defined by a correlation coefficient (R) which ranges between –1 and +1 where a value of +1 indicates perfectly positive correlation and –1 indicates perfectly negative correlation.

Spreadsheet tools such as Microsoft Excel provide add-ins or features that can be used to calculate the correlation coefficient (R) between the variables.

Best Use:

Testing a hypothesis where it is believed that two factors have a relationship of some kind such whether the occurrence of one factor might lead to another.

How To Use:

1. Identify which two factors will be analyzed (e.g. Incident Ticket counts and Request For Change (RFC) ticket counts)

2. Gather data on each variable to be analyzed (e.g. Incident and RFC counts by month)

3. Input into a spreadsheet table

4. Add the Analysis ToolPak Add-In to your Excel File

5. Analyze data using a Correlation Analysis tool within the spreadsheet (e.g. This tool can be found under the Tools menu by selecting "Data Analysis" (Tools > Data Analysis > Correlation Analysis) in Microsoft Excel.

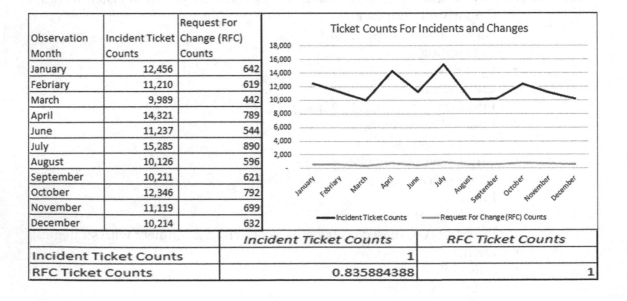

Observation Month	Incident Ticket Counts	Request For Change (RFC) Counts
January	12,456	642
Febriary	11,210	619
March	9,989	442
April	14,321	789
June	11,237	544
July	15,285	890
August	10,126	596
September	10,211	621
October	12,346	792
November	11,119	699
December	10,214	632

	Incident Ticket Counts	RFC Ticket Counts
Incident Ticket Counts	1	
RFC Ticket Counts	0.835884388	1

Crawford Slip List

Description:
This tool can be used to quickly solicit many ideas for a solution to a problem or issue without spending time on discussion or requiring others to give up decision-making authority.

Best Use:
Quickly generating a large number of creative ideas and solutions to a problem or issue from a large group.

How To Use:
1. Ahead of time, construct a formal problem statement of the issue to be addressed
2. Convene a workshop to address the issue
3. Hand out index cards (about 20-30 per team member)
4. Read the formal problem statement to the group
5. Ask team members to write down as many ideas as they can think of that will solve the problem – one idea per index card and no discussions allowed
6. In 5-10 minutes, collect the cards
7. Dismiss the team
8. Use a small appointed group of staff or managers to sort through the ideas that were presented for some creative ideas to solve the issue.

Example:

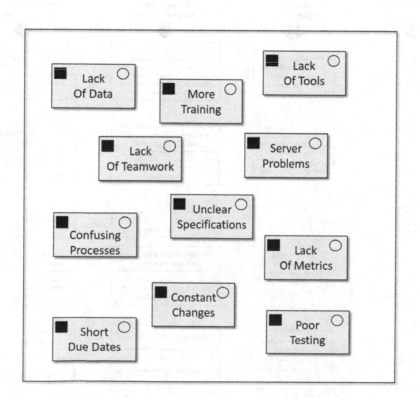

Critical-To-Quality (CTQ) Tree

Description:
This tool builds a diagram that can be used to understand what is important to the business customer. It helps translate unclear, undefined, high-level customer wants or needs into tangible requirements with measurable quality metrics.

Best Use:
Creating a thorough understanding of business/customer needs and identifying what kinds of quality data to collect and measure.

How To Use:
1. Establish a meeting or workshop to build the CTQ Tree.
2. Create a high-level statement expressing the overall need of the business customer.
3. Build diagram from left to right starting with output desired by the business customer
4. Identify key drivers that create value for the output desired by the business customer
5. Identify what will be measured to validate that the drivers are successful
6. Identify thresholds by which those measurements will indicate success or failure

Example:

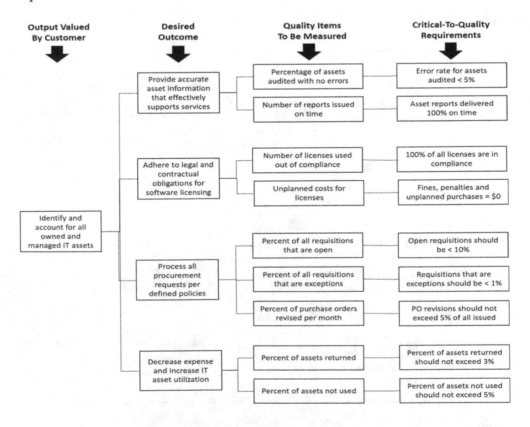

Data Collection Plan

Description:
This tool provides a structured plan that outlines the types and sources of data that need to be collected in order to comprehensively understand the current state of a problem or issue to test for hypothetical underlying causes.

Best Use:
Creating a thorough understanding of business/customer needs and identifying what kinds of data to collect to resolve underlying issues and problems.

How To Use:
1. Enter each hypothesis into the tool
2. Enter the appropriate data needed to prove each hypothesis
3. Enter a target date to collect data by
4. Identify an owner who will be responsible for gathering the appropriate data (Note: Data can come from systems, interviews, or team observations)
5. Rank the importance of each hypothesis by how critical each individual piece of data is to testing the designated hypothesis
6. Add in any additional comments as needed
7. Track progress of the plan in the status column

XREF	Importance	Hypothesis	Data Needed	Data Source	Date Due	Owner	Status	Comments
01	High	Unapproved changes	Incident ticket descriptions	Incident Ticket System	mm/dd/yyyy	PJ	Not Started	xxx...
02	Moderate	People errors	Incident ticket descriptions	Incident Ticket System	mm/dd/yyyy	RS	In Process	xxx...
03	High	Lack of communication about changes	Attendance records from CAB meetings	Change Management System	mm/dd/yyyy	DF	In Process	xxx...
04	Low	Lack of skills	Skills assessment results	Learning Management System	mm/dd/yyyy	HM	Not Started	xxx...
05	High	Poor testing of applications	Application test results	Testing Logs	mm/dd/yyyy	LP	In Process	xxx...
06	Moderate	Hardware failures	Incident tickets categorized as hardware failures	Incident Ticket System	mm/dd/yyyy	PJ	Complete	xxx...
07	Moderate	Software failures	Incident tickets categorized as software failures	Incident Ticket System	mm/dd/yyyy	PJ	Complete	xxx...
08	Moderate	Network failures	Incident tickets categorized as network failures	Incident Ticket System	mm/dd/yyyy	RS	In Process	xxx...

Data Selection Sample

Description:
This tool can be used to select data observations from a group in which those observations can be used to represent the entire group population.

Best Use:
Gathering data on service, process, hardware or software operating performance when capture of all data is not feasible or can be done (e.g. cannot monitor a service end to end or collection of system trace data would create disruptive system issues or performance times).

How To Use:
1. Identify the data to be collected
2. Identify a sampling technique to be used (see below)
3. Identify how sampled data will be interpreted along with any assumptions that might be used.

Depending on the nature of the issue being studied, different sampling techniques may be more appropriate than others. If sub-populations vary considerably, it may be better to sample each subpopulation independently.

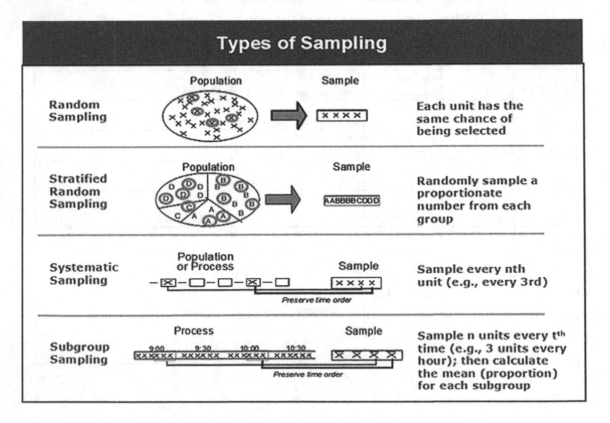

Design Of Experiments (DOE)

Description:
This tool provides a systematic procedure that is carried out under tightly controlled conditions to discover an unknown effect, to test a hypothesis or to illustrate a desired effect.

Best Use:
Testing different hypotheses or "what if" conditions in a tightly controlled manner to determine a future course of action or to discover an underlying cause.

How To Use:
1. Define the problem
2. Determine the objective
3. Brainstorm focus areas
4. Design the experiment
5. Ensure a capable and repeatable measurement system is being used
6. Conduct the experiment
7. Watch for unexplained errors and noise factors
8. Analyze data
9. Do not confuse correlation with causation
10. Interpret results
11. Verify results and refocus the experiment if necessary

A high level process for conducting DOE is outlined below:

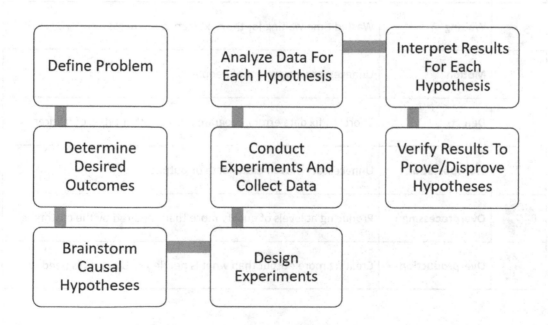

Eight Deadly Wastes

Description:
This tool can be used to analyze a process by examining each process step to see if it falls into one of the categorizations of eight different types of non-value added activities, or waste.

Best Use:
Identifying non-value add activities for a given process, technology solution or service.

How To Use:
1. Diagram a process into its steps
2. For each step, determine the extent to which it includes each type of waste as shown in the table below
3. For each step with a type of waste identified, identify changes that would remove the waste from the step
4. Assemble identified changes into an overall action plan to improve the process.

	Type Of Waste	Description
	Inventory	Excess products and materials that are not being used
	Talent	Improper or inefficient use of people skills and knowledge
	Waiting	Wasted time waiting for the next step in a process
	Motion	Unnecessary movement of people
	Defects	Efforts to fix data errors, program bugs or other types of failures
	Transportation	Unnecessary movement of data or outputs
	Overprocessing	Producing at levels of quality more than required by the customer
	Overproduction	Creating more output than what is needed or before it is needed

Failure Mode and Effects Analysis (FMEA)

Description:
This tool provides an approach to prioritize potential process, technology, availability, or other service defects based on their severity, expected frequency and likelihood of detection. It highlights weaknesses in the service, technologies or processes in terms of the customer. The resulting analysis is used to identify probable courses of correction such as design improvement, coding changes, solution delivery changes or process improvements.

Best Use:
Prioritizing and setting action plans to address the most important risks of a process, technology or service that must be addressed.

How To Use:
1. Brainstorm all possible process failure modes
2. Assign values for each of the following: severity, probability of occurrence and probability of detection (1 – 10 with 10 being the worst value)
3. Calculate a risk preference number by multiplying the failure mode values together
4. The risk preference number (RPN) becomes the prioritization indicator and highlights the failure modes that must be prevented from occurring.
5. Develop actions to prevent occurrence of the failure modes

FAILURE MODE AND EFFECTS ANALYSIS (FMEA)				
Server Install Process		Type: ⟨ Process ⟩ Technology Service		
Failure Mode	A) Severity (Rate 1-10 with 10 = Most Severe)	B) Probability Of Occurrence (Rate 1-10 with 10 = Highest Probability)	C) Probability Of Detection (Rate 1-10 with 10 = Hardest To Detect)	Risk Preference Number (RPN) (Score as A x B x C))
Slow performance	5	4	3	60
Wrong configuration	9	2	8	144
High number of failures	2	3	4	24

Fault Tree Analysis

Description:
This tool can be used to visualize a top down, deductive failure analysis in which an undesired state of a service or process is analyzed using Boolean logic to combine a series of lower-level events.

Best Use:
Getting to root cause for complex issues such as why a process is under-performing.

How To Use:
1. Define the undesired process to study
2. Obtain an understanding of the process, inputs, outputs, key objectives
3. Inventory symptoms and unwanted events of the process
4. For each unwanted event, work backwards to identify contributing events that when they all occur can cause the leading event
5. Construct the fault tree in a manner as shown below
   a. Each unwanted event is at the top of the fault tree map
   b. Contributing events are shown a lower levels
6. Evaluate the fault tree
7. Address the causes identified.

Example:

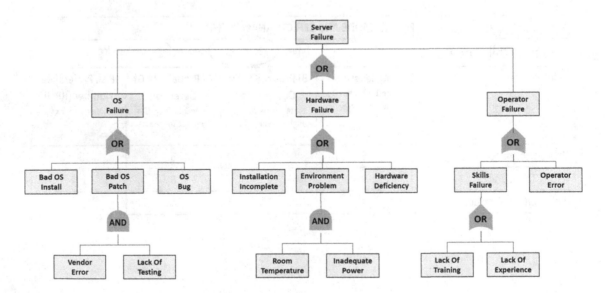

Five Whys

Description:
This tool provides a facilitation method which allows a project team to "peel away" the layers of process symptoms and uncover the root cause of a problem by asking "why" a number of times. It is called "Five Whys" because five is a good rule of thumb for the number of times continuous improvement teams should ask "why" when given answers to ensure that the root cause has been properly identified.

Best Use:
For quickly getting to the real root cause of a problem or issue.

How To Use:
1. Identify the issue or problem under study
2. Ask 'Why" the issue or problem occurred and solicit an answer
3. Ask again "Why" that answer occurred
4. Keep asking "Why" for each answer given – usually 4-5 "Whys" will drill down to the real root cause.

Example:

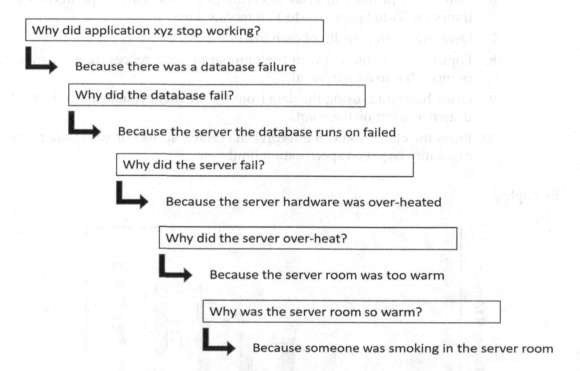

Why did application xyz stop working?

Because there was a database failure

Why did the database fail?

Because the server the database runs on failed

Why did the server fail?

Because the server hardware was over-heated

Why did the server over-heat?

Because the server room was too warm

Why was the server room so warm?

Because someone was smoking in the server room

Histogram

Description:
This tool allows process or service data observations, collected over a period of time, to be displayed graphically in such a way as to present its frequency in a bar chart form. The resulting display can show relative frequency of occurrences, centering, or shape of the distribution of the data. It indicates shifts and can answer basic questions around process or service capabilities.

Best Use:
For understanding the impact of process or service deficiencies and making decisions around which aspects of a process to improve or act upon.

How To Use:
1. Determine the observations to be measured
2. Collect and record a reasonable amount of data over specified period of time
3. Create a frequency table
4. Count the number of data points
5. Determine range of data (max. – min.)
6. Determine number of class intervals (e.g. Less than 50 points = 5 to 7 intervals, 50-100 points = 6 to 10 intervals. Etc.)
7. Determine range width of each interval
8. Populate each interval with the number of occurrences (how many data points fall into each interval
9. Draw histogram using the data from the frequency table. Each interval is drawn as a bar on the chart.
10. From the chart, you can interpret the center, spread or variation, process capability based on specification limits, etc.

Example:

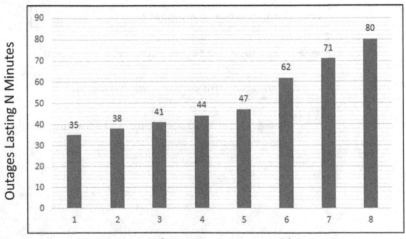

Frequency Of Outages By Range Of Minutes

Improvement Process Roadmap

Overview:

Provides a framework for project activities to undertake lean improvements. Columns can serve as high level project steps where data in each column can serve to highlight the key activities and outcomes.

Best Use:

Providing a common repeatable framework of activities for making lean improvements.

How To Use:

1. Structure a project plan using the column headers as key milestones or phases

2. Populate the plan with steps and deliverables taking from the Key Activities and Key Outcome Examples as shown in the chart

3. Customize the activities and deliverables to the specific improvement being addressed

	Define	Measure	Analyze	Improve	Control
Objectives	• Identify the problem • Define customer requirements • Set improvement goals	• Validate the problem • Measure current state performance • Identify opportunity areas	• Identify the root causes of waste • Develop high level designs to address inefficiencies and issues	• Develop detailed solutions to address the root causes • Build, test and implement solutions	• Confirm inefficiencies have been addressed • Launch, monitor and continuously improve
Key Activities	• Scope and plan the project • Develop SIPOC • Understand the stakeholders (VOC) • Prioritize and select key areas to measure (data collection plan)	• Measure key areas and defects • Gather detailed VOC • Determine critical to quality (CTQ) requirements • Identify and prioritize opportunity areas	• Root cause analysis • Develop and validate hypotheses • Define financial impact and develop business case • Develop conceptual designs	• Develop solutions • Design detailed future state • Conduct pilots • Implement quick hits • Deploy change management programs	• Implement future state • Monitor progress • Identify areas for continuous improvement • Monitor benefits

	Define	Measure	Analyze	Improve	Control
Key Outcome Examples	• Project Charter • Financial Driver Analysis (EVM) • SIPOC • Voice of Customer (VOC) • Critical to Quality (CTQ)	• As-Is Process/ Value Stream Mapping • Non-Value Added Analysis • Data Collection and Sampling • Cycle Time Analysis • Pareto Analysis	• Cause and Effect Diagrams • Root Cause Analysis (5 Why's) • Failure Modes and Effects Analysis • Organizational Alignment	• To-Be Process/ Value Stream Mapping • Standard Work • Poka-Yoke • 5 S • Visual Workplace • Change management	• Control plans • Scorecards and control charts • Business case

Issue Log

Description:
This tool can be used to capture, manage, and track issues that are identified throughout a continuous improvement project. Potential issues may be related to timelines, resources, stakeholders, and the implementation of solutions.

Best Use:
Tracking and managing improvement project issues.

How To Use:
1. As the improvement project is executed, issues that arise should be input into the spreadsheet shown below in the Description column
2. Additional information on each issue should also be entered including who owns the issue, and the potential impact of the issue to the project
3. The Issue Log should be reviewed on a frequent basis by the project team
4. Issues and their resolution progress should be reported on by the project manager on a regular basis
5. Once the issue has been resolved, the Issue Log should be updated indicate a closed or completed status.

Example:

XREF	Importance	Hypothesis	Data Needed	Data Source	Date Due	Owner	Status	Comments
01	High	Unapproved changes	Incident ticket descriptions	Incident Ticket System	mm/dd/yyyy	PJ	Not Started	xxx...
02	Moderate	People errors	Incident ticket descriptions	Incident Ticket System	mm/dd/yyyy	RS	In Process	xxx...
03	High	Lack of communication about changes	Attendance records from CAB meetings	Change Management System	mm/dd/yyyy	DF	In Process	xxx...
04	Low	Lack of skills	Skills assessment results	Learning Management System	mm/dd/yyyy	HM	Not Started	xxx...
05	High	Poor testing of applications	Application test results	Testing Logs	mm/dd/yyyy	LP	In Process	xxx...
06	Moderate	Hardware failures	Incident tickets categorized as hardware failures	Incident Ticket System	mm/dd/yyyy	PJ	Complete	xxx...
07	Moderate	Software falures	Incident tickets categorized as software failures	Incident Ticket System	mm/dd/yyyy	PJ	Complete	xxx...
08	Moderate	Network falures	Incident tickets categorized as network failures	Incident Ticket System	mm/dd/yyyy	RS	In Process	xxx...

Kaizen Program

Description:

This tool can be used to focus attention on ongoing improvement that involves small improvements being made on an ongoing basis. Over time these small improvements can produce changes every bit as dramatic as the "big project" approach. Big gains are achieved through many small efforts over time.

Best Use:

Operating an ongoing Continuous Improvement Program where budgets are limited and there is a desire to get everyone involved. Also acts as a great morale lifter and empowers staff to get heard and make changes.

How To Use:

1. Establish and communicate a Continuous Improvement Program by which every support staff member will be involved in a small way.

2. Each member is challenged to identify at least one small improvement every 2-4 weeks that they think will provide some benefit.

3. Establish a Continuous Improvement Register to record improvements recommended.

4. Establish a governance or oversight team that meets on a regular basis to review each improvement and determine which ones suggested should go forward.

5. Establish recognition and rewards for support staff that come up with best ideas for improvement.

Recommended improvements should be small in nature and easily doable. Some criteria for the kinds of improvements that could be suggested are:

1. Requires minimal or no funding to implement

2. Can be implemented by support staff or management with no more than 2 hours per week in effort

3. Does not require a formal project to be setup and approved

4. Little data gathering is required

5. Anything goes – not just small technical changes but could also include process changes, changes in responsibilities, and building of a small support aid such as a spreadsheet, form, small script or other document.

Kanban Board

Description:
This tool can be used to visually present a workflow of tasks and enable improvement teams to optimize the flow of their work. Physical Kanban boards, like the one pictured below, typically use sticky notes on a whiteboard to communicate status, progress, and issues.

Best Use:
Focusing a team on the necessary tasks needed to complete a project or build effort. These especially work well with project teams that may be using agile approaches in their project efforts.

How To Use:
1. Create lanes on the board and label them with a step in the team's process (to do, plan, etc.).
2. Cards are then placed on the board in lanes that indicate the current status of the work.
3. Optionally, you can use card colors to demonstrate the type of work being done (e.g., purple for a service feature to be developed, green for a program bug to be fixed, etc.), or priority (e.g. Red for urgent, green for normal priority, etc.).
4. Assign each card to a single team member who will be accountable for the task to be done.
5. Post the board somewhere where it can be easily seen by support staff and management.
6. Update the board with current status of tasks (adding or removing tasks as needed) on a regular basis. Many projects may do this daily.

Example:

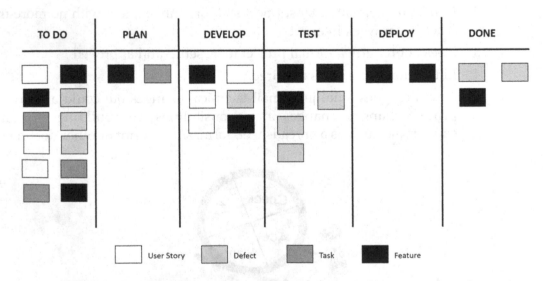

Each ticket posted includes a Ticket ID, Description of User Story, Defect, Task or Feature to be implemented , who owns the ticket and a rough labor estimate in hours

Kano Analysis

Description:

This tool can be used to classify and prioritize customer requirements based on their impact on customer satisfaction.

Best Use:

Identifying which features in a service or product will have the most impact on customer satisfaction or reason to buy.

How To Use:

1. Brainstorm and generate a list of customer requirements.
2. Determine which category each requirement falls into:
   a. *Dissatisfier/Basic Expectations:* Customer's minimal expectations. Doing them well does not guarantee success, but doing them poorly will put you out of business.
   b. *Satisfier/Performance Wants:* Creates rising satisfaction the more they are fulfilled, but also lead to increasing dissatisfaction the less they are fulfilled
   c. *Delighter/Exciters:* Factors or features that go beyond customer's expectations
3. State and review the company's business objective
4. Determine and prioritize which customer requirements should be focused on.

Example:

Kano Diagram Of Customer Requirement Impact On Customer Satisfaction

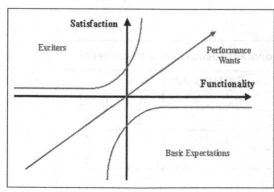

Example Kano Analysis

Email Support Service	
Customer Requirement	**Type**
Send/Receive Messages	Satisfier
Large Mailbox Space	Satisfier
Prompt Support	Dissatisfier
Managed Mail Backup	Delighter
Calendaring	Satisfier
Large Font Sizes	Satisfier
Recover Deleted Email Messages	Dissatisfier
Signatures and Emoticons	Delighter

Nominal Group Technique

Description:

This tool can be used to help a team come to a consensus opinion when dealing with a number of issues. This approach permits the full team to rank the issues in terms of importance and consolidates the ranking to one prioritized listing.

Best Use:

Gaining group consensus on a direction to take when there are multiple issues and opinions about what to do next. This technique works well when conducting brainstorming sessions.

How To Use:

1. Review the overall issues and problems to be addressed
2. Have each team member generate one action item
3. Post and review each action item submitted to make sure everyone understands the item
4. Continue in round-robin fashion across all team members until a list of action items has been generated
5. Group action items into general categories
6. Each team member then gets 10 "sticky dots" to be used as votes
7. Each team member then "spends" their dots on the action items they feel are most important to be prioritized first (they can spend one or more dots on any action item)
8. Identify the top action items – those with the most dots
9. Sort and rank the top action items
10. Finalize a priority ranking and discuss with the team

Example:

Which Solution Aspects Should Development Focus On Most This Year?						
		Participants				
ID	Item	#1	#2	#3	#4	Total
1	Sales distribution system	3			1	4
2	Brand		1			1
3	Financial strength			3		3
4	Customer loyalty					
5	Social media					
6	Leadership team		2	2	3	7
7	Project management	2				2
8	Product development			1		1
9	Customer service center					
10	Software Systems	1	3		2	6

Non-Value Step Analysis

Description:
This tool can be used to identify the steps of a process or workflow for efficiency by categorizing each step into value or non-value.

Best Use:
Generating improvement focus and improvement opportunities for the potential flow across a process or value stream.

How To Use:
1. Identify a process to be reviewed for waste
2. Identify and chart out all the steps in the process. You may use an already constructed process map or value stream map.
3. Classify each step in one of three categories:
   a. Value-adding: A step that adds value in the eyes of the external customer
   b. Value-enabling: A step that allows the process to do work for the external customer more quickly or effectively
   c. Non-value adding: A step that does not add value to the process in the eyes of the external customer
4. Examine and review those steps categorized as Value-Enabling or Non-Value Adding:
   a. Are these steps necessary?
   b. Can the process be executed without them?
   c. Do they create non-value work for the customer?
   d. Are they repetitious of other steps (e.g. copying data from one place to another)
5. Examine and review the Value-Adding steps
   a. Can these be done more efficiently?
   b. Can they be automated?
6. Make a list of action items to address un-needed steps or improve the process.

Example:

Non-Value Step Analysis: Change Management Process		
Step	Action	Analysis
01	Draft Request For Change (RFC)	Value-Enabling
02	Submit RFC TO Change Management	Value Enabling
03	Review RFC Form For Completeness	Non-Value Adding
04	Escalate RFC For Review	Non-Value Adding
05	Review RFC For Potential Risks	Value-Adding
06	Escalate To Change Advisory Board	Non-Value Adding
07	Approve Change	Non-Value Adding
08	Schedule Change	Value-Enabling
09	Notify RFC Owner Of Approval	Value-Enabling
10	Validate Success/Failure Of Change	Non-Value Adding
11	Conduct Post Implementation Review	Value-Enabling

Observation Post

Description:
This tool can be used to deal with intermittent issues that appear to happen randomly or appear to come and go and cannot be recreated or repeated.

Best Use:
Complex issues where a sequence of events needs to be assembled to determine exactly what contributes to them.

How To Use:
1. Identify the issue to be monitored for
2. Identify the symptoms or observed events that will trigger assembly of an observation team
3. Identify support staff who will respond when the issue triggers occur
4. Upon trigger of the event, assemble staff to monitor real-time events to gather evidence for possible causes
5. Implement specialized monitors, traces, system dump actions, or logs of user activities as needed to provide data for observations
6. Monitor events and catch in real-time to identify possible causes for the problem.

Many times for this kind of tool you would set up the procedures to quickly assemble a team and capture observable data. These procedures are then quickly evoked at the point that the issue appears.

Organizational Change Flow Of Activities

Description:

This tool provides a quick approach for framing organizational change activities. These activities are used to prepare users for acceptance and use of a new system or solution.

Best Use:

Implementation and deployment projects where the deployed solution will present a new way of working and operating and there is a concern about resistance to the new approach.

How To Use:

1. Identify stakeholders impacted by the new solution
2. Group stakeholders into types (e.g. administrators, managers, sales, support, etc.)
3. Inventory what each stakeholder type needs to know about the new system
4. Group inventory into campaigns – logical groupings of items to be communicated e.g.

   a. Awareness Campaign – what's new, why, how it will impact people, next steps
   b. Learning Campaign – training for use of the new system or solution
   c. Validation Campaign – tests and games to ensure new skills have been learned
   d. Support Campaign – where to get help, user hotline, reference sources, etc.

5. Establish success indicators for campaigns (e.g. 90% of staff can recite benefits)
6. Identify communication events for each campaign (e.g. solution overview, demo)
7. Identify how each event will be delivered (e.g. video, train-the-trainer, classroom course)
8. Schedule events and campaigns in line with project schedules
9. Agree plans and events
10. Execute on the agreed communication plan

Key Communications Operating Principles	
Adoption and Learning	Conduct a series of workshops that repetitively introduces stakeholders to new skills and ways of working
Resistance Management	Allow stakeholders time to get comfortable with the new solution via hands-on use of tools, case examples, walkthroughs and opportunities to raise questions and concerns
Transition Readiness	Give stakeholders an opportunity to demonstrate their new skills and walk them through the transition approach step by step
Stakeholder Management	Maintain an inventory of stakeholders and target knowledge and training for each stakeholder type – monitor stakeholder progress through each campaign to validate readiness for transition

The Organizing ITSM book (Trafford Press ISBN: 978-1-4907-6270-8) provides a great reference if more detail on building a program of organizational change is desired.

Organizational Change Success Factors

Description:
This tool provides an inventory of key success factors for any Organizational Change effort.

Best Use:
Assessing the effectiveness of an organizational change initiative or laying out the key factors that must be in place for a successful organizational change initiative.

How To Use:
1. Review organizational change plans and activities
2. Identify key concerns and issues with the current or planned Organizational Change Program approach
3. Assess each step in those plans against the critical success factors presented below
4. Identify program gaps and issues that need to be overcome
5. Update plans or change strategies to address any factors found to be missing

Organizational Change Success Factors are:

 Compelling Business Case For Change. The reason for the change is clearly understood and there is general agreement that the change is important enough to spend time and money on.

 Leadership Commitment. Leaders actively are seen participating in the change. They are "walking the talk" and acting to champion the change, not just leaving it up to subordinates to lead and communicate.

 Stakeholder Commitment. Stakeholders are committed to spending time and budget on making the change happen. They accept responsibility for making the change happen and actively participate in the program.

 Organizational Alignment. The organizational structure, roles, processes and systems are in place to effect the change. Skills and culture are aligned to support the future state vision that will be achieved by the change.

 Shared Vision. The vision for the change is shared across all leadership and stakeholders. A resistance plan is in place to manage those who do not accept or understand the change. Leadership and stakeholders can recite a consistent message and talking points about the change.

 Effective Communication. A change communications strategy in in place to build awareness for the change, communicate progress towards the change and answer the "what's in it for me" question.

 Skills Attainment. A training plan, program and set of activities is in place to provide people with the right skills and knowledge to transition to the target state vision and operate once it is implemented.

 Progress Measurements. Metrics are in place to provide transparency for change progress and results achieved. Reports and dashboards are in place to communicate results to leadership and all stakeholders.

 Change Architecture. Appropriate processes, tools, people and systems are in place to support transition activities towards the change. Existing infrastructure and systems do not impede change progress.

 Change Transition. A clear set of change implementation and deployment plans are in place. A deployment strategy and approach is in place and has been communicated and accepted by leadership and stakeholders.

Pain Value Analysis

Description:
This tool can be used to identify and prioritize which service or process issues and deficiencies cause the most pain to the business.

Best Use:
Uncertainty over which issues or deficiencies should be addressed first. Identifying those issues that impact the business the most.

How To Use:
1. Develop a list of issues and deficiencies
2. For each issue or deficiency:
   a. Identify number of people affected
   b. Identify duration of issue or deficiency
   c. Identify the business impact
   d. Estimate business costs related to the issue or deficiency (e.g. unplanned labor, lost sales, fines, penalties, etc.)
3. Weight each issue by above factors
4. Plot results out on a chart like the example shown below
5. Identify the top issues to focus on first.

Example:

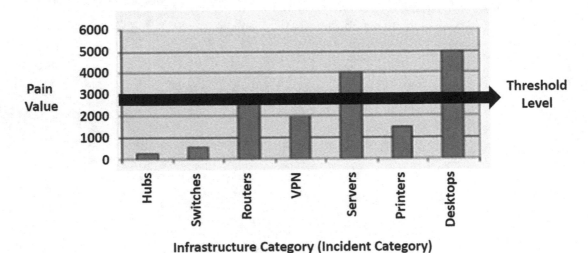

Pareto Analysis

Description:

This tool can be used to provide a data graphing analysis that focuses on identifying the top 20% of sources that result in 80% of the problems.

Best Use:

Situations in which there is uncertainty about where to start for issues that have multiple causes. Can also be useful when trying to find a root cause of an issue or separating the most important potential causes of issues from more trivial ones.

How To Use:

1. Identify the problem or issue to be solved
2. Gather data regarding that problem and the various factors that may be affecting it
3. Form a table listing the data and the frequency as a percentage
4. Arrange the rows in the decreasing order of importance of the causes, i.e. the most important cause first
5. Add a cumulative percentage column to the table
6. Select the top causes for the problem - the highest frequency of occurrence indicates the sources with the greatest opportunity for improvement.

Example:

Top Causes

Service Failure			
Causes	% of total	Computation	Cumulative %
Network controller	35	0+35%	35
File corruption	26	35%+26%	61
Addressing conflicts	19	61%+19%	80
Server OS	6	80%+6%	86
Scripting error	5	86%+5%	91
Untested change	3	91%+3%	94
Operator error	2	94%+2%	96
Backup failure	2	96%+2%	98
Intrusion attempts	1	98%+1%	99
Disk failure	1	99%+1%	100

Pick Chart

Description:

This tool can be used to provide a visual means for organizing lists of ideas and identifying which ones will provide the most benefit. The Pick Chart is a quadrant (as shown below). The meanings of each quadrant area are:

- **Possible** - ideas that are easy to implement but have low value
- **Implement** - ideas that are easy to implement and provide high value
- **Challenge** - ideas that are hard to implement and difficult to determine what value might be obtained
- **Kill** - ideas that are hard to implement and have low value.

Best Use:

After brainstorming sessions to identify which ideas that were generated during the sessions can be implemented easily with the most benefits.

How To Use:

1. Gather the list of ideas
2. Put ideas on cards – one idea per card
3. Create and post the Pick Chart template (as shown below)
4. Read out each idea to the group to ensure it is understood
5. Post the card in one of the quadrants as agreed to by the group
6. Repeat steps 4-5until all the ideas have been posted
7. Discuss and agree which ideas the group should go forward with.

Example:

	High Value	Low Value
Easy To Implement	Implement	Possible
Hard To Implement	Challenge	Kill

Principled Negotiation Method

Description:

This tool can be used to provide a constructive approach when negotiating. It focuses on a positive set of activities that can result in a win-win for both sides versus traditional bargaining where each side conceals their real motives and takes positions.

Best Use:

Any negotiation situation where there is a desire to have both parties resolve their differences in a positive manner.

How To Use:

1. In advance of negotiations, have both parties review and agree the rules as shown in the table below
2. Operate negotiating sessions with the rules that have been agreed upon
3. During the course of negotiations, if it is determined that the rules are being violated, state that fact to both sides and take actions to bring negotiations back on course.

Negotiating Rule	Negotiating Actions
Separate people from the problem	• Allow each side to state their emotions in a matter-of-fact manner (e.g. no yelling or using provocative speech that can easily anger the opposite side). • Listen well to the other side. • Try to understand why the other side may be emotionally upset and how that happened.
Focus on interests and not positions	• Communicate your real interests and what each side hopes to achieve • Avoid (at all costs) hiding your real interests, stating a position, and then expecting to be pushed to a fallback position • Trust on both sides – do not treat each other's interests as positions
Invent Win-Win Options	• Both parties should focus on creative solutions that give the most to both parties • Do not treat created solutions as positions
Agree measures	• Use standard measures that both parties can agree on (e.g. what the real budget available is) • Do not turn measures into negotiating positions

Prioritization Matrix

Description:
This tool can be used to prioritize a list of items and to organize areas of focus or solutions as part of a continuous improvement project. It can be included as part of the Continual Service Improvement (CSI) Register to prioritize improvement activities and projects or simply identify which ones should go into the register.

Best Use:
Determining and selecting the specific improvement activities to work on next as part of a Continual Service Improvement Program.

How To Use:
1. Identify the criteria against which prioritization will be conducted and agree as a team
2. Develop a rating scale to be used (e.g. values 1-10)
3. Develop a weighting value for each criteria
4. List the action items to be prioritized
5. Have each team member individually rate each action item against the criteria
6. Compile the results
7. Multiply the criteria ratings and weightings together to get a score for each action item
8. Rank each action item in descending order by their scores
9. The highest scoring items determine which areas the team should focus on or what solutions should be pursued.

Example:

All Identified Opportunities	Business Alignment 1=Low 3=Medium 9=High	Information Availability 1=Low 3=Medium 9=High	Expected Benefits 1=< $100,000 3=$100-$500K 9=> $500,000	Ease Of Execution 1=Complex 3=Moderate 9=Easy	Time To Implement 1=>9 Months 3=3-9 Months 9=<3 Months	Weighted Score	Decision Accept > =100 Reject < 100
Criteria Weight	20%	20%	20%	20%	20%	100%	
Develop a specifics form for all Parking Application request tickets	9	9	3	3	3	437.4	Accept
Provide support teams with access to HIPPA secure screens and data	9	3	3	3	1	48.6	Reject
Update Problem Management in the ITSM tool to allow link from problem ticket to multiple changes (versus only one)	3	3	3	9	3	145.8	Accept
Implement a dashboard for service owners	3	3	3	3	3	48.6	Reject
Etc.							

Process Lead Time Analysis

Description:
This tool can be used to benchmark the current state of a process and uncover potential inefficiencies. Process and lead time are defined as:

Process Time: The actual time it takes to complete an activity or the total amount of time spent working on a specific activity

Lead Time: The elapsed time associated with completing an activity; i.e. total duration.

Best Use:
Determining if large differences exist between process and lead times which could indicate process down time or waiting time which is a type of waste.

How To Use:
1. Identify the process to be analyzed
2. Inventory the activities that support that process
3. Identify how much average time is spent actually executing each activity
4. Identify the duration of time spent from the point the activity is initiated to when it hands off to the next activity (may require interviews with actual process participants)
5. Calculate the percentage of lead time as process time / lead time
6. Smaller percentage values may indicate opportunities to eliminate waste from the process.

Example:

Process: Incident Management – Level 1				
Activity	**Execution Time in Minutes**	**Total Task Time in Minutes**	**Lead Time Percentage** (Execution / Total Task Time)	**Waste Candidate** (Yes = Lead time < 90%)
Capture incident ticket (Start)	0.0	0.0	100.0%	No
Transfer ticket to Level 1 support	0.1	1.0	10.0%	No
Review ticket	5.0	5.0	100.0%	No
Research issue	10.0	10.0	100.0%	No
Escalate ticket	1.0	1.0	100.0%	No
Resolve ticket	60	90	67.0%	Yes
Close ticket (End)	2.0	30.0	7.0%	Yes

Process Mapping

Description:

This tool can be used describe how work flows through the organization, displaying each task or operation that is performed to complete the end to end process. Process diagrams can be at different levels of detail such as: Process, Sub-process and activity level.

Best Use:

Providing a structured visual means that enables cross functional teams to see and understand how the real process works or should work.

How To Use:

1. Identify the process to be mapped
2. Agree standard flow charting symbols that will be used to identify the process
3. Create horizontal lanes to represent process roles that will execute the process
4. Optionally, add in lanes for any external processes that provide input or receive output
5. Optionally, add in a lane for any tools that will be used as part of the process
6. Identify each step in the process along with decision points and specific outputs
7. Link steps to external processes and tools where these may be used.

Maps can be developed using an existing flow diagram or from scratch, individual or team generated. The resulting map should be reviewed for completeness and accuracy by team members representing all functions and possibly departments.

Example:

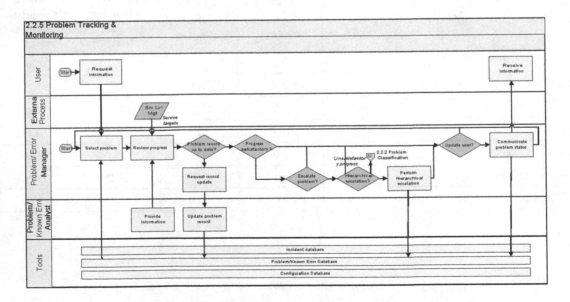

Regression Analysis

Description:

This tool can be used to predict the value of a variable based on the value of two or more other variables. It can be used for predicting and forecasting a future state situation based on how that situation has been historically behaving.

Best Use:

Modeling the impacts of an issue if it is not addressed and emphasizing to executive management what might happen if nothing is done.

How To Use:

Regression formulas can get quite complex. A method for doing this is presented in detail in a separate chapter in this book (See Modeling Future State chapter).

Alternatively, you can use a free Tooling Aid provided in ITSMLib in the ITSM Metrics and Reporting section.

Example:

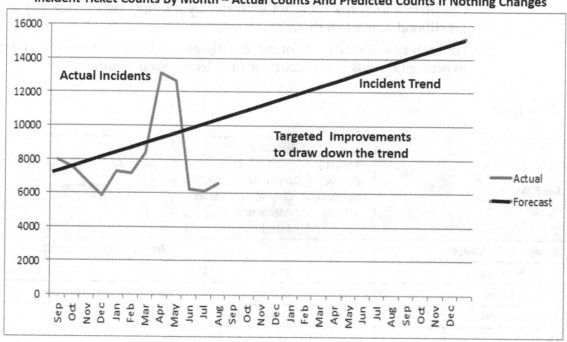

Risk Mitigation Matrix

Description:
This tool can be used to help teams understand the risks associated with solutions or changes being proposed, prioritize those risks, and develop plans to minimize the impact of those risks.

Best Use:
Identifying risks involved with continual service improvement projects regardless of size and level of complexity.

How To Use:
1. Identify and inventory each risk placing them in the leftmost column of the matrix.
2. Identify the severity of each risk in terms of its impact on the business organization or project using the suggested scoring as shown in the example.
3. Identify the likelihood that the risk might occur using the suggested scoring as shown in the example.
4. Calculate a total risk score for each risk by multiplying the Severity and Likelihood scores together.
5. For each risk, identify one or more mitigation actions that could be taken to prevent the risk from occurring or at least lessen its impact.

Example:

Key Risks	Impact (1=Low, 2=Medium, 3=High)	Likelihood Of Occurrence (1=Low, 2=Medium, 3=High)	Total Risk Score	Mitigation
Stakeholder resistance	3	2	6	Bring in executive support
Hardware failure	1	1	1	n/a
Software failure	2	2	4	Keep software up to date
Application failure	3	2	6	Increase testing activities
Etc.				

SIPOC Diagram

Description:
This tool can be used to display a high-level flow that displays cross-functional activities in a single, simple diagram. It provides an "at-a-glance" perspective of the process steps incorporating suppliers, inputs, process, outputs, and customers ("SIPOC"). Accommodates processes of all sizes and even entire organizations.

Best Use:
Creating an initial starting point in understanding how a process works.

How To Use:
1. Identify the process to be diagrammed
2. Define its scope (where does it start and end?)
3. Name the suppliers, inputs, outputs, and customers
4. Identify the process major process activities and group like activities together, placing each major step in order in a block diagram.

Example:

Supplier	Input	Process	Output	Customer
Change Management	• Forward Schedule of Changes (FSCs) to determine when incidents may be resolved • Approval and coordination of RFCs submitted by Problem Management for change to resolve Known Errors and problems	• Provide error control • Conduct major problem reviews	• RFCs submitted for problems and Known Errors that require a change • Validation that problems have not recurred for Known Errors that have been resolved via Change Management • RFCs for handling standard changes used to resolve Known Errors • Identification of criteria for successful changes • Participation in post implementation reviews • Participation on the Change Advisory Board (CAB)	Change Management

Record and Classify Problem Ticket → Assign Problem Management Team → Determine Root Cause → Determine Work Around → Submit Request For Change (RFC) → Remove Error → Conduct Post Problem Review

Stakeholder Map

Description:
This tool can be used to identify and assess the importance of key people, groups, or organizations that may significantly influence or be affected by the implementation of a new service, process or technology product.

Best Use:
Provides a first step towards development of communications strategies to get support, reduce obstacles, or reduce resistance to a solution being implemented.

How To Use:

1. Generate a list of all potential stakeholders
2. Review the list and identify the interest and/or influence that each stakeholder will have in the solution
3. Prioritize and rate the stakeholders interest/influence
4. Publish all information for the team to refer to when making decisions
5. Strategize how to approach each stakeholder to gain their support and reduce future obstacles.

Example:

Name	Title	Type	Priority	Acceptance	Influence
Jim Jones	VP of IT Architecture	Senior Management	Contact Immediately	Positive	Decision Maker
John Smith	Manager, Sales Operations	User	Contact Immediately	Champion	Influencer
Becky Thomas	VP, Sales	Customer	Contact in 4 weeks	Neutral	Influencer
Rachel Marrow	VP, Service Delivery	Sponsor	Unknown	Unknown	Unknown
Ralph Johnson	Business Representative	Customer	Contact in 3 months	Neutral	Subject Expert
Siddrah Kumar	VP, IT Operations	Senior Management	Unknown	Against	Controller

Storyboard

Description:

This tool can be used to quickly obtain ideas from a large group to identify the root cause of a problem and create an action plan to address it.

Best Use:

Quickly pulling together a complete story of the problem definition, potential causes, root cause, improvement options, recommended solution and action plan for an issue or problem.

How To Use:

1. Assemble the team or group
2. Discuss symptoms and observations seen with a particular issue or problem
3. List team member hypotheses as to what root cause may be
4. Discuss and agree the root cause
5. Give team members some amount of time to individually identify their ideas (typically 10-15 minutes) as to what steps to take to remove the root cause
6. Have each team member present their ideas, in round robin fashion, one at a time
7. Record each idea on flip chart, making sure it is understood and making no criticism or judgment
8. Review and consolidate the list grouping activities identified into steps
9. Reorder the steps identified into a logical progression
10. Agree the progression of steps and activities
11. Formalize an action plan for moving forward using a template like the one below:

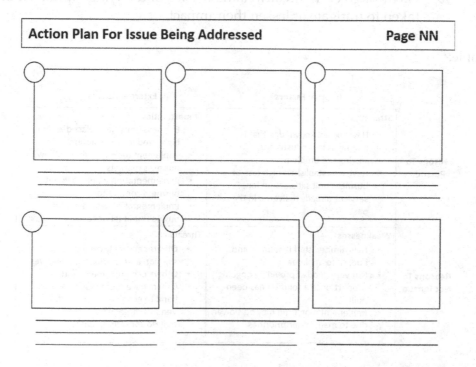

SWOT Analysis

Description:
This tool can be used to provide a structured planning method to evaluate a new service or product that will be produced or to determine the course of a strategic set of actions. SWOT stands for Strengths, Weaknesses, Opportunities, and Threats. A SWOT meeting allows participants to creatively brainstorm, identify obstacles and strategize possibly solutions to the obstacles identified.

Best Use:
Any decision-making situation when trying to determine the viability of a service, product or correction action. Also for situations where it is desired to assess a current state situation for weaknesses and threats to identify mitigation actions to lessen them.

How To Use:
1. Establish a workshop or meeting that will review the objective being decided upon
2. Explain the SWOT chart (shown below) so there is common understanding of what goes in each quadrant
3. Develop an initial SWOT with the entire group at a high level
4. Break the group into smaller teams
5. Have each sub-team fill out the SWOT in more detail for 30-60 minutes
6. Reconvene the group
7. Have each sub-team present their SWOT to the rest of the group
8. Record the sub-team SWOTS by merging them with the larger SWOT done earlier
9. Go through each threat/weakness listed and identify options that could be taken to mitigate or lessen their impact.

Example:

	Internal Factors	External Factors
Reasons To Pursue	**Strengths** • Have expert knowledge that is unique in the industry for solving the problem • Have an established high rate of business unit satisfaction for services already delivered in the past	**Opportunities** • Business units have placed a very high need for the solution • Implementation would open new business markets • Implementation would lock out business competitors • Implementation would save on business unit labor costs
Reasons To Not Pursue	**Weaknesses** • Have limited staff resources and budget to implement • Not very good at providing ongoing support once a solution has been built • Implementation time may be slower due to many other priorities	**Threats** • Others can easily copy the solution and provide it themselves • Others can implement faster • Others have more resources at hand to get things done faster • Vendors already have products that do something similar

Value Stream Map

Description:

This tool can be used to visualize and understand how value flows (e.g. physical, organizational and informational flows) into and through a process and how information facilitates the flow. Value streams can be done for an as-is for a current state process and/or a future state process.

Best Use:

Situations where waste needs to be identified in a process. Can also be used to provide a structured means for characterizing physical flow of work, information and materials through the customer value stream for a current process, a future process or both to show a comparison of value.

How To Use:

1. Select the process to be mapped
2. Define what value is from the customer's view (price, speed, quality, accuracy, etc.)
3. Collect data (process steps, execution times, wait times, etc.)
4. Map the current state of the value stream.
5. Identify waste in the current value stream (See Process Lead Time Analysis tool)
6. Map the future process state and develop a transition plan to this future state.

Example:

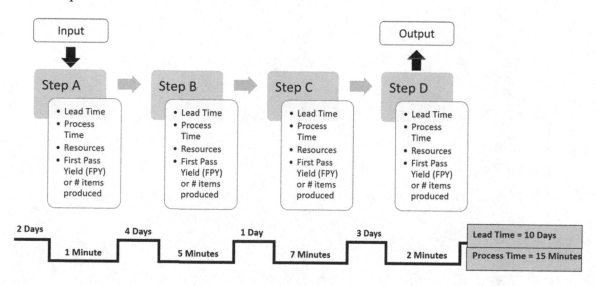

About the Author

Randy A. Steinberg has extensive IT Service Management and operations experience gained from many clients around the world. He authored the ITIL 2011 Service Operation book published worldwide. Passionate about game changing management practices within the IT industry, Randy is a hands-on IT Service Management expert helping IT organizations transform their IT infrastructure management strategies and operational practices to meet today's IT challenges.

Randy has served in IT leadership roles across many large government, health, financial, manufacturing and consulting firms including a role as Global Head of IT Service Management for a worldwide media company with 176 operating centers around the globe. He implemented solutions for one company that went on to win a Malcolm Baldrige award for their IT service quality. He continually shares his expertise across the global IT community frequently speaking and consulting with many IT technology and business organizations to improve their service delivery and operations management practices.

Randy can be reached at RandyASteinberg@gmail.com.